Fresh food cooking with

Seafood

R&R PUBLISHING PTY LTD

CONTENTS

Introduction to Seafood

Australia's waterways offer flavours to complement every occasion, from a casual barbecue to a formal dinner, and everything in between.

In addition to offering a wealth of flavours, seafood is affordable, easy to prepare and endows a wide range of health benefits on those who eat it.

Nowhere is the size and diversity of Australia more obvious than in its wide range of seafood. Australian waters boost hundreds of seafood species, and more than 300 of these are harvested by commercial and recreational fishers. On any day the Sydney Fish Market has more than 100 species for sale.

Seafood is part of the Australian experience. Fish was a major part of the diet for Aboriginal and Torres Strait Islander communities before colonisation. Settlers from the United Kingdom brought with them their knowledge of

northern hemisphere species, and until after World War II sea mullet and barracouta were the most popular fish.

In the late 1940s and 1950s, when Greek and Italian migrants arrived in Australia and commercial fishing operations began in earnest, Australians began to appreciate the vast range of seafood afforded by the country's estuaries, rivers, lakes and 36,000 kilometre-coastline.

Seafood is an integral part of the Australian lifestyle. Whether we are enjoying a sizzling summer day, or in the middle of winter, we will choose a seafood dish to complement the occasion. Nowadays our tastes have broadened from those of the first colonials. Australians favourite seafood include octopus, crab, lobsters and prawns. With increasing numbers of Asian migrants, Australians are discovering previously unheard-of seafood, and learning new ways to cook it.

That is one of the beauties of Fresh Food Cooking with Seafood. It offers traditional European recipes as well as Asian and modern Australian dishes. Fresh Food Cooking with Seafood breaks down many of the perceived barriers people have about cooking with seafood. Simple step-by-step pictures show the ease with which any type of seafood can be prepared for cooking. Because these recipes incorporate seafood they are not only tasty but healthy.

Australians are increasingly conscious of the importance of sensible eating habits, and seafood is an important element to include in a well-balanced diet. Seafood averages less than 2 per cent fat; an extremely low level. This is lower than most chicken cuts and much lower than lean red meat. Seafood is particularly good for those on low-fat diets.

Research shows that eating fish two or three times a week can help lower cholesterol and reduce the risk of heart disease.

Seafood is good news for slimmers. All seafood is low in kilojoules, with fewer kilojoules than even the leanest meat or chicken. And, of course, with seafood you don't need to trim any fat. Just grill, barbecue, bake, steam, poach or microwave seafood to keep a low kilojoule count.

Seafood is an excellent source of top quality protein and minerals, including iodine, zinc, potassium and phosphorus. It is also rich in vitamins, especially the B group.

The small amount of fat in fish is rich in Omega-3-fatty acids, making fish a great heart food. Omega-3-fatty acids from fish can stop blood clots forming and blocking off arteries, thus reducing the risk of heart attack.

Recent studies show that eating seafood reduced joint stiffness and pain from rheumatoid arthritis, and that consumption of fresh, oily fish was associated with a significantly reduced risk of asthma in children.

Sydney Fish Market is the hub of the Australian fishing industry. Prices achieved at the Market's Monday-to-Friday auction are the benchmark for seafood prices across the whole country.

But the Market is more than an auction. It houses the country's largest seafood retailers, develops marketing programmes for seafood, and is home to the Sydney Seafood School and Fish Line.

From its inception in 1989 the role of the Sydney Seafood School has been to promote seafood. The School runs a variety of cookery classes hosted by its own demonstrators and top Australian chefs. At these classes guests learn how to buy, handle and prepare seafood to create quick and tasty meals. After a demonstration, guests move into the practical kitchen and recreate the dish for themselves before enjoying this with an appropriately matched glass of wine.

Another Sydney Fish Market service is Fish Line, a free seafood cookery advice service available to anyone who has questions about how to buy, store, prepare or cook seafood. Please call Fish Line on 02 9552 2180 to have any questions about seafood answered.

Fresh Cooking with Seafood gives Australians more reasons to enjoy seafood. Enjoy the recipes and savour the flavours of this country's abundant array of seafood.

Alain Albert, of the Katkoko Cafe Creole, Enmore Road, Newtown, Sydney.

Buying and Storing Fish

When buying fish for your family, make sure it is fresh and, if you plan to freeze it, don't buy fish that has already been frozen. There are a few points to look for to tell if fish is fresh:

- it should not have a strong odour, but should have a pleasant and mild 'sea' smell;
- the flesh should be firm with a smooth, slippery skin and no yellow discolouration;
- whole fish should have bright eyes and red gills.

If you are worried about your children swallowing bones, you should look for the many cuts available without bones. Try flake (also boneless hake), swordfish, marlin, tuna, blue grenadier, sea perch, jon dory, tail-pieces of ocean trout, ling, blue eye cod and salmon. You will also find that many fish-mongers now sell de-boned fillets such as salmon and trout.

If the fish has been packed in a plastic bag, unwrap it as soon as you get home and place it in a glass or stainless steel dish.

Cover lightly and keep in the coolest part of the refrigerator.

Use as soon as possible and, if not using the next day, place over a pan of ice.

If freezing, wrap fillets individually for easy separation. Always defrost in the fridge or microwave, or cook from frozen. Never thaw at room temperature and never refreeze thawed fish.

Preparing Fish

The two types of fish are described as flatfish and roundfish. Both types need to be cleaned before use, but cleaning procedures vary.

Scaling and Finning

Most fish will need to be scaled. However, there are a few exceptions such as trout, tuna, shark, leatherjacket and others described in the text of this book.

When poaching a whole unboned fish, it is best to leave the dorsal and anal fins attached. This will to help hold the fish together during cooking. Rinse fish.

Wash fish and leave wet as a wet fish is easier to scale. Remove scales using a knife or scaler and start at the tail and scrape towards the head.

Clip the dorsal fin with scissors or, if desired, remove both the dorsal and anal fins by cutting along the side of the fin with a sharp knife. Then pull the fin towards the head to remove it.

Gutting

Gutting techniques are different for roundfish and flatfish. When preparing fish to bone or fillet, remove the entrails by gutting through the belly. If you wish to serve the fish whole, preserve the shape of the fish by gutting through the gills.

Roundfish

For boning or filleting, cut off the head behind gill opening. Use a sharp knife and cut-open belly from head to just above anal fin. Remove membranes, veins and viscera. Rinse thoroughly.

To preserve shape of roundfish, cut through the gills, open outer gill with the thumb. Put a finger into the gill and snag the inner gill. Gently pull to remove inner gill and viscera. Rinse well.

Flatfish

To gut, make a small cut behind gills and pull out viscera.

Skinning

The tasty skin of some fish enhances the flavour. However, other fish have strong or inedible skin which interferes with the flavour. Always leave skin on when poaching or grilling a whole fish.

Roundfish

When skinning a whole roundfish, make a slit across the body, behind the gills, with another just above the tail. Then make another cut down the back.

Flatfish

Use a sharp knife, start at the tail and separate the skin from the flesh. Pull the knife towards the head, whilst holding the skin firmly with the other hand. Do not 'saw' the knife.

Skin the whole flatfish, by first turning the dark side up and then cutting across the skin where the tail joins the body. With a sharp knife, peel the skin back towards the head until you have enough skin to hold with one hand.

Anchor the fish with one hand and pull the skin over the head. Turn fish over and hold the head whilst pulling the skin down to the tail.

Cutting Fillets, Steaks & Cutlets

Fillets are pieces of boneless fish. Steaks & cutlets are cross sections cut from the whole fish. There are slightly different techniques in filleting roundfish and flatfish.

Roundfish

With a sharp knife, make a slit along the backbone from head to tail, and then make a cut behind the gill.

Hold the head and insert the knife between fillet and ribs. Slide knife along the ribs (do not use a sawing motion), and cut down the length of the fish. Remove fillet by cutting off at the anal fin. Repeat on the other side of fish.

Flatfish

Skinning a fillet

Place skinned fish on chopping board with eyes up. Cut from head to tail through the flesh in the middle of the fish to the backbone. Insert a sharp knife between the ribs and the end of the fillet near the head. Pull knife down the fillet on one side of the backbone and remove.

Cut off the remaining fillet in the same manner. Turn fish over and remove the two bottom fillets.

Place fillet skin side down and cut a small piece of flesh away from the skin close to the tail. Hold skin tight, and run a sharp knife along the skin without cutting it.

Cutting a Steak or Cutlet

Using a solid, sharp chef's knife, cut off head just behind the gills. Slice the fish into steaks or cutlets of the desired thickness.

Buying and Preparing Shellfish and Crustaceans

A diverse and astonishing variety of univalves (abalone), bivalves (oysters, clams, mussels), crustaceans (crabs, prawns and lobsters) and cephalopods (squid and octopus) is available for our cooking-pot. There is one point of concern, however, and that is the fact that once out of water, shellfish deteriorate quickly.

Opening Bivalves

All bivalves, oysters, clams and mussels should be tightly closed when purchased.

If you wish to use the shells in cooking, it is best to scrub them with a stiff brush under cold, running water.

Oysters

If you use technique rather than strength, oysters are easy to open. It is best to hold the unopened oyster in a garden glove or tea towel (which will protect one hand from the rough shell) whilst you open the shell with an oyster knife, held in the other hand.

Hold the oyster with the deep cut down and insert the tip of the oyster knife into the hinge, then twist to open the shell. Do not open oyster by attempting to insert the oyster knife into the front lip of the shell.

Clams

To open clams it is best to use a blunt clam-knife to avoid cutting the meat. Try freezing bivalves for half an hour to relax the muscles—they will be easier to open.

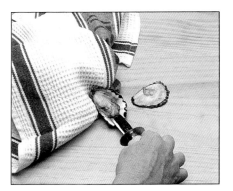

Slide the clam-knife inside upper shell to cut the muscle that attaches it to the shell. To serve, discard the upper part of shell and cut muscle under bottom half, then replace oyster into half-shell.

Slide blade of the clam-knife between the two halves of the shell. Work knife toward hinge until shell parts.

Slide blade along inside of one shell to cut connecting muscles; then do the same to other side to dislodge flesh.

Mussels

The threads of tissue that protrude from the mussel shell are called the byssus, or, more commonly, the beard. As mussels die quickly after debearding, it is best to prepare them immediately. Use the same technique for opening as a clam.

Cleaning Crabs

The most common crabs sold in Australia and New Zealand are the blue swimmer, mud crab, spanner crab and Morton Bay bug. Southern king crab or Alaskan king crab are also available, but not in huge quantities.

Hard-Shelled Crabs (Mud Crab)

Wash and scrub under cold, running water. When clean, the entire crab may be poached or steamed. However, as most mud crabs are sold live, if you wish to cook the crab, you must first kill and disjoint it, and then remove the edible parts.

To kill crab instantly, stab just behind the eyes with the point of a sharp knife. Another killing-technique is to place crab in freezer for a few hours.

Place crab on its back, and gently fold back tail flap or apron. Twist and pull apron off. You will find that the intestinal vein is attached and will pull out along the apron. Discard.

Hold the crab with one hand where the apron was removed. Use the other hand to pry-up, and tear-off and discard the top shell.

Remove the gills, take out the greyish bag and pull out mandibles from front of crab.

Hold the body where the legs were attached and apply pressure so that crab splits in half along the centre of the body. Fold-back halves and twist apart.

Twist-off claws and legs where they join the body. Crack with hammer or nutcracker to make the meat easy to remove.

Soft-Shell Crabs (Blue Swimmers)

Cut across the eyes with a sharp knife. Pull out and discard the stomach sac. Turn over and lift the flap or apron and fold it away from the body. Pull out the apron and attached intestinal-vein, and discard. Turn crab right-side-up and lift flaps on each side near legs. Scrape-off and discard spongy gills.

Abalone

Using a strong knife, force the blade tip into the thin part of the shell underneath the flesh. Fork blade backwards and forwards until muscle is freed from shell. Lift out flesh, remove intestine and wash flesh well under cold, running water.

Slice-off dark heel (sucker pad). Slice the flesh horizontally in two, wrap slices in tea-towel and pound well with the side of a meat-mallet or cleaver until limp and velvety. Slices can be cut in thin strips or chopped, depending on cooking method.

Prawns

Most people prefer to remove the head and body-shell before eating. However, the entire body of the prawn is edible, depending on the cooking method.

To peel, break-off head, place finger on underside between legs, and roll prawn. The body shell will come away. Then squeeze tail-section and remainder of shell will slip off.

Slit down the middle of the outside curve and it will expose the intestinal vein. Remove it, and wash prawn under cold, running water. It is not necessary to remove the vein from bay or smaller prawns. However, larger prawns vein sometimes contain shell or grit which can interfere with the taste of the recipe.

Yabbies

Fresh water crayfish or yabbies can be found in many inland streams. They have very sweet meat in the tail. Normally cooked in their shells.

To remove the intestinal vein, hold on a firm surface, right-side-up.

Hold firmly with one hand and pull the tail flap away from the yabby to remove the intestinal vein.

Squid

Squid can be poached, sautéed, fried, stuffed, baked and grilled. Do not overcook squid as it will become tough.

Rinse in cold water and then cut off tentacles, just above the eye. Squeeze the thick centre-part of the tentacles. This will push out the hard beak, which you should discard.

Squeeze the entrails out by running your fingers from the closed to the open end. Pull out the quill and discard.

Peel-off skin by slipping finger under it. Pull-off the edible fins from either side and also skin them.

Lobster (Southern Crayfish)

You can purchase lobster, whole-live, whole-frozen and whole-cooked. Also available are uncooked frozen lobster-tails and canned or frozen lobster-meat.

To kill a live lobster, hold it on its back on a firm surface. With a heavy chef's knife, stab the point into the mouth to sever the spinal cord. You may also stun the lobster by placing it in the freezer for a period (about 30 minutes for each 500g).

Weigh to calculate cooking time. Place lobster in a large pot of cold, salty water and bring to simmering point. Simmer, but do not boil, for 8 minutes per 500g weight.

Hold lobster right-side-up on a firm surface. Pierce the shell at the centre of the body behind the head.

Cut lobster in half lengthwise and remove and discard sac near the head and intestinal vein in the tail. Remove any roe from the body and reserve for flavouring sauces.

Clean the lobster by rinsing under cold, running water.

Octopus

Cut head from body section, just below the eyes, to remove tentacles. Cut-out eyes and clean body cavity. Push beak up through centre of joined tentacles, cut-off and dispose.

Wash thoroughly. Pay particular attention to tentacles as the suckers may contain sand.

Skin is difficult to remove from fresh octopus. Skin may be left on for cooking. However, to remove skin, parboil in a little water for 5–10 minutes, then skin when cool enough to handle.

To clean small, whole octopus, cut-up back of head and remove gut. Push beak up and cut-out. Cut-out eyes and wash thoroughly.

ATLANTIC SALMON

Atlantic Salmon is the marketing name (Salmon)

Different from the many species of 'Pacific Salmon' which are available in the North American market (often canned). Also different from the 'Australian Salmon', which is more correctly a 'Sea Perch'.

Availability: A farmed fish (mainly in Tasmania, Australia). Spawned in fresh water and farmed in salt water. Available most of year but more abundant from July to April. Sold whole and in fillets, steaks, and cutlets (chilled, frozen, smoked or vacuum-sealed). Roe is also available.

Storage: Scale, gill and clean whole fish. Best refrigerated by wrapping in GLAD Wrap or stored in airtight GLAD Snap Lock Bags. Refrigerate for 2–3 days (or freeze for up to 6 months).

Preparation: Best served rare after quick sealing on a very hot grill. Try wrapping in green leaves such as banana leaves, silverbeet or lettuce. Also can be covered with your favourite herbs and baked enclosed in GLAD Foil.

Cooking: Can be steamed, poached, smoked, baked, pan-fried, grilled or barbecued. Also used for sashimi. Because of its taste and texture, Atlantic Salmon suits most flavourings. Due to its excellent flavour and texture, this fish is widely used for mousseline, finfish pâtés, terrines and roulades, or as a stuffing for white finfish in seafood cannelloni and lasagne.

Barbecued Atlantic Salmon (whole)

Ingredients
1 Atlantic Salmon (1.5–2kg)
salt
MasterFoods Black Peppercorns (freshly ground)
lemon juice
1 tablespoon butter (softened)
olive oil

Method
1. Rinse salmon under cold running water and pat dry (inside and out). Sprinkle cavity with salt, pepper and lemon juice.

2. Stuff with Summer Garden Stuffing (recipe follows), skewer and lace closed; then rub generously with softened butter.

3. Tear off double thickness of OSO Aluminium Foil (as long as, and twice the width of, the salmon). Oil one side. Use skewer to punch a dozen holes through foil.

4. On barbecue, place foil flat on grill (oiled side-up) and place salmon on foil. Measure the thickest point, and allow total cooking time of 12–15 minutes per 2.5cm.

5. Halfway through allocated cooking time, gather long edges of foil together to form a 'handle'. Grip the 'handle' and flip salmon. Re-open foil for rest of cooking time.

6. Fork-test for 'doneness' along both sides of the backbone at thickest point. Juices should run clear, and flesh should be opaque.

Note: The recipe may also be used for baked salmon. Measure at thickest point, and bake at 230°C for 10 minutes per 2.5cm-thickness (or until juices run clear, and the flesh, fork-tested along the backbone, is opaque).

Serves 4

Summer Garden Stuffing

Ingredients
1 medium potato (boiled, finely chopped)
1 medium tomato (finely chopped)
½ small cucumber (finely chopped)
2 tablespoons red capsicum (finely chopped)
2 tablespoons onion (finely chopped)
125g prawn or crabmeat (chopped)
2 teaspoons lemon juice
1 teaspoon MasterFoods Dill Leaf Tips (finely chopped)
salt and pepper

Method
1. In a bowl, combine all ingredients, tossing gently and thoroughly (to distribute evenly).

2. Stuff salmon cavity lightly.

Note: Any remaining stuffing may be wrapped in GLAD Foil and cooked alongside salmon.

Salmon with Lime Butter

Ingredients
4 salmon cutlets
1 tablespoon lime juice
1 tablespoon lime rind (grated)
2 teaspoons MasterFoods Parsley Flakes
125g butter (softened)
3 tablespoons butter (extra)

Method
1. Melt extra butter in frying pan, add cutlets, and cook over a moderate heat (for about 3 minutes each side).

2. Serve cutlets with lime butter spooned on top.

3. **Lime butter:** Combine lime juice, lime rind, parsley and softened butter.

Serves 4

Jan's Handy Tip
When lemons or limes are in season, squeeze them into a GLAD Ice Cube Bag and freeze. This will give you exact portions of juice for use in recipes—one ice cube makes one teaspoon of juice. Also great for storing stock—saves filling up all your ice cube trays, and easier to store.

Grilled Salmon Fillets

Ingredients

4 x Atlantic Salmon fillets
250mL dry red wine
125mL olive oil
125mL lemon juice
2 shallots (chopped)
2 teaspoons MasterFoods Freshly Crushed Garlic
1 teaspoon MasterFoods Freshly Chopped Ginger
1 teaspoon salt
½ teaspoon MasterFoods Rosemary Leaves
¼ teaspoon Tabasco
4 large capsicum rings
4 large slices white onion

Serves 4

Method

1. Rinse salmon under cold running water, pat dry, and set aside.
2. In shallow glass bowl, combine all but last two ingredients. Place salmon in marinade. Cover, and refrigerate for 1–2 hours.
3. Remove from refrigerator and bring to room temperature. Remove salmon from marinade and reserve the liquid.
4. Cook salmon, capsicum and onion on well-oiled barbecue (or grill over medium heat) for 6–7 minutes (or until lightly browned).
5. Baste with marinade, turn, and baste again. Continue cooking for another 5 minutes (or until flesh is opaque when fork-tested).
6. To serve: top fillets with capsicum and onions.

BARRAMUNDI
Barramundi is the marketing name

Has a large mouth with projecting lowerjaw and strong tail. Has white tender and firm flesh with a large flake, and a mild distinctive taste. Sought by anglers because of its fighting qualities.

Availability: Most fresh barramundi is caught and consumed by anglers. In the eastern States it is generally available in frozen fillets. When purchasing fresh whole barramundi, look for firm flesh, clear bulging eyes and a pleasant sea-smell.

Storage: Clean whole fish, then wrap well in GLAD Wrap. Wrap fillets in GLAD Wrap and store in refrigerator for 2–3 days (or in freezer for 3–6 months).

Preparation: Depending on size, can be cooked whole, but scoring is essential. When using thick fillets, score first. Barramundi should be skinned before cooking.

Cooking: Allow 750g of fillets for 4 serves. Poach, grill, shallow-fry, bake, barbecue or microwave. Season with a selection of ginger, chives, lime, lemon, orange juice and rind, basil, tarragon, dill, rosemary, thyme, garlic, peppercorns, parsley.

Barramundi Fillets, Mussel and Lemon Butter Sauce
Ingredients
250mL dry white wine
1 small carrot (cut into 1cm-cubes)
1 small onion (cut into 1cm-cubes)
½ stick celery (cut into 1cm-cubes)
1kg black mussels
1 teaspoon MasterFoods Ground Turmeric
125g butter
juice of ½ lemon
black pepper (freshly ground)
4 whole baby barramundi (deboned, leave skin on; each should weigh about 500g)
olive oil
½ teaspoon lemon juice (extra)
steamed *bok choy* (for serving)

Method
1. In a medium saucepan, bring the wine, carrot, onion and celery to the boil. When the liquid begins to boil, add mussels, and continue to boil (until the mussels open). Remove from the pot, take meat from shell, and set aside.

2. Use half the remaining liquid to make a butter sauce. Strain liquid, add turmeric, return to heat, and allow to boil. Turn heat down, and whisk in butter and lemon juice. When simmering, add mussel meat and freshly ground black pepper.

3. Pan-fry barramundi fillets in a shallow frying pan in olive oil (for about 3–4 minutes each side). When fish is turned, dribble lemon juice over it.

4. Serve with steamed *bok choy* on a plate (fish on top), and with mussels and sauce poured over.

Serves 4

Jan's Handy Tip
Wild-caught barramundi are larger than farmed barramundi. Barramundi yield thick, boned-out fillets which can be served whole, or as an attractive cutlet. The large flakes provide good-sized portions, and the firm texture makes it a versatile finfish with which to work.

Barramundi with Fresh Tarragon Sauce
Ingredients
4 barramundi fillets
plain flour
2 eggs (lightly beaten)
125g dry breadcrumbs
oil (for shallow frying)

Tarragon Sauce:
30g butter
2 tablespoons MasterFoods Tarragon Leaves (chopped)
1 tablespoon garlic
1 tablespoon chives (chopped)
1 teaspoon lemon juice
1 teaspoon MasterFoods Original Dijon Mustard
85mL brandy
125mL cream

Method
1. Coat fillets in flour, and then in eggs and breadcrumbs. Heat oil in frying pan, and add fillets. Fry, turning once, until fish is cooked through.

2. **Sauce:** Heat butter in a small saucepan. Add tarragon, garlic, chives, lemon juice, mustard and brandy. Simmer uncovered for 2–3 minutes. Gradually stir in cream. Reheat sauce. Do not boil.

Serves 4

Barramundi with Garlic and Tarragon butter
Ingredients
8 baby barramundi fillets
250g butter
6 teaspoons MasterFoods Freshly Crushed Garlic
½ bunch fresh tarragon leaves (chopped)
juice of 2 lemons
crusty bread (for serving)

Method
1. Grill fish for 3 minutes each side (until cooked)

2. Dice butter and cook over low heat with garlic, tarragon and lemon juice. Do not allow butter to burn.

3. Pour over fish fillets, and serve with crusty bread.

Serves 4

Barramundi Putanesca

Ingredients

Sauce:

4 teaspoons olive oil
1 large onion (finely diced)
2 teaspoons MasterFoods Freshly Crushed Garlic
2 teaspoons MasterFoods Tarragon Leaves
1 tablespoon MasterFoods Tomato Paste
125mL white wine
400g tomatoes (whole, peeled)
4 anchovy fillets (chopped fine)
125g pitted olives

4 barramundi fillets (approximately 200g each)

Serves 4

Method

1. Preheat oven to 180°C.

2. Heat olive oil in a saucepan. Add onion and garlic, and cook (until onion is transparent).

3. Add tarragon and tomato paste, and stir for 3–4 minutes. Add wine, tomatoes, anchovies and olives, and cook (until tomatoes have broken up).

4. Cut 4 pieces of OSO Aluminium Foil into 30cm-squares. Place foil shiny side-down, and put fillet in the centre.

5. Spoon sauce mixture on top of fillet. Bring opposite sides of foil together and roll (until closed).

6. Place in oven (at 180°C) for approximately 25 minutes.

BLACKFISH

**Luderick is the marketing name
(Luderick, Nigger, Black Bream, Darkie)**

Small head, sub-terminal mouth. Prominent scales. Dark olive-green to brownish with 5–8 dark vertical bands. Reasonable table fish. Flesh white, moist and soft, with a distinct flavour.

Availability: Normally found in coastal reefs, estuaries and shallow flats with abundant green weed. Best table size: 500g–1kg.

Storage: Bleed on capture, and fillet and skin as soon as possible. Wash fillets in sea water, wrap well in GLAD Wrap, and store in refrigerator for 2–3 days (or freezer for 3–6 weeks).

Preparation: Scale, skin and clean. Best to fillet and remove tough skin; the fat layer will come away with the skin.

Cooking: Use a dry method as flesh is oily. Shallow- or dry-fry; best if fried in bread crumbs. Can be baked or barbecued, wrapped well in OSO Aluminium Foil. Season with garlic, curry, Chinese Five Spice, Cumin, ginger, basil, lemon and lime juice and rosemary.

Blackfish Risotto

Ingredients
1 tablespoon MasterFoods Cajun Seasoning
1 tablespoon cornmeal
700g blackfish fillets
1 tablespoon olive oil
1 tablespoon olive oil (extra)
1 onion (chopped)
1 teaspoon MasterFoods Freshly Crushed Garlic
400g arborio rice
200mL white wine
700mL basic fish stock (page 39; simmering)
4 medium tomatoes (finely chopped)
2 tablespoons MasterFoods Tomato Paste
1 jalapeño chilli (finely chopped)
2 tablespoons butter
3 tablespoons sour cream (optional garnish)
¼ bunch fresh Italian parsley (chopped; for garnish)

Method
1. Mix the Cajun spice and cornmeal together, and toss the fish in the mixture (until well coated). Heat one tablespoon olive oil, and cook the fish (until the flesh is opaque and the coating is fragrant). Set aside.
2. In a separate high-sided frypan, heat the extra olive oil, and sauté the onion and garlic (until softened). Add the rice, and stir to coat.
3. Add the wine, and simmer (until the liquid has been absorbed). Add simmering stock (a ladle at a time), and stir well. Do not add further stock until liquid has been absorbed.
4. Add tomatoes, tomato paste and jalapeño chilli, and combine.
5. Continue adding stock (a ladle at a time), stirring well after each addition, and allowing all the liquid to be absorbed before the next addition of stock is added.
6. When all the stock has been added, return the fish and all its juices to the risotto, and combine gently. Add the butter and mix well.
7. Serve in individual bowls. Garnish with a dollop of cream and fresh herbs. Serve immediately.

Serves 4

Thai Blackfish

Ingredients
4 teaspoons red curry paste
200mL coconut milk
dash of MasterFoods Sweet Thai Chilli Sauce
cream
4 blackfish fillets (roughly chopped)
1 medium-sized eggplant (diced)
8 baby corn
1 bunch fresh basil (chopped)
boiled rice
1 sprig fresh basil (for garnish)

Method
1. Add curry paste to saucepan on medium heat. Stir in coconut milk, chilli sauce and dash of cream.
2. Bring sauce to simmer, and then add fish, eggplant, corn and basil. When cooked, serve on some boiled rice, and garnish with fresh basil.

Serves 4

Cajun Blackfish Fillets with Cucumber Raita

Ingredients
To prepare fish:
1 jar MasterFoods Cajun Seasoning
6 tablespoons MasterFoods Ground Paprika
¾ tablespoon rock salt
4 medium blackfish fillets
125mL olive oil

Cucumber Raita:
250g natural yogurt
1 cucumber (seeded and peeled)
½ teaspoon MasterFoods Mint Flakes
juice of 1 lemon
½ red capsicum (finely diced)
salt and pepper

Method
1. Mix all fish-preparation ingredients together (except fish and olive oil), and sprinkle on large plate.
2. Press blackfish fillets on Cajun spice mix on either side (until covered).
3. Heat frypan with olive oil, and cook each side (for approximately 8 minutes).
4. **Cucumber Raita:** Mix all ingredients together, and season with salt and pepper.

Serves 4

Jan's Handy Tip
The recipes for Blackfish in this section are reasonably spicy. You will therefore need to accompany your dish with a compatible wine. My suggestion here is Stoneleigh Sauvignon Blanc, from the wonderful Marlborough region in New Zealand.

Chargrilled Blackfish with Chive Oil and Polenta

Ingredients

1kg blackfish fillets
baby rocket leaves (for serving)

Chive Oil:

100mL extra virgin oil
2 bunches fresh chives (chopped)
pinch rock salt
pinch MasterFoods Black Peppercorns (freshly ground)

Polenta:

30g butter
1 small onion (finely chopped)
800mL milk
90g polenta
salt
MasterFoods Black Peppercorns (freshly ground)

Method

1. **Chive Oil:** Mix all ingredients together, and set aside (for at least 4 hours). Ideally make the chive oil a day before use.

2. **Polenta:** In a medium-sized saucepan, heat butter and onion for 2–3 minutes (until onion loses colour), pour in milk, and bring to boil. Whisk in the polenta (until thickened), and season to taste with salt and pepper.

3. Season fish, and brush with olive oil. Chargrill until just cooked.

4. Serve by spooning soft polenta on a serving plate, add fish and drizzle chive oil over the top. Place baby rocket leaves around fish.

Serves 4

Jan's Handy Tip

Whilst fish is grilling, take 6 Romano tomatoes, cut lengthwise, and roast in oven at 140°C (until soft). These can then be placed on the serving plate around fish with the rocket leaves (as photographed).

BLUE EYE

Blue Eye is the marketing name (Big Eye, Deep Sea Trevalla, Trevalla, Blue Eye Cod, Sea Trevalla, Blue Nose, Warehou, Bonita, Blue Bream, Stone Eye [NZ])

A deep water fish with pale, pink flesh and mild, delicate flavour. Is moist with firm texture and medium-to-large flakes. A very popular table-fish with only a few bones (which are easily extracted).

Availability: Most of year, but more abundant in summer. Available whole, and in both fillet- and cutlet-form. Smoked roe is available in some areas.

Storage: Remove skin, gill and clean. Best refrigerated by wrapping in GLAD Wrap or stored in airtight container. Refrigerate for 2–3 days (or freeze for up to 6 months).

Preparation: Skinless fillets can be cubed and coated individually in batter or crumbed herbs. Ideal fish for serving as finger-food.

Cooking: Can be steamed, poached, smoked, baked, fried, grilled or barbecued; also suited for sashimi. Because of its taste and texture, Blue Eye suits most flavourings.

Marinated Grilled Blue Eye Cod

Ingredients
lemon juice (extra)
water
4 blue eye cod cutlets
125mL lemon juice
2 tablespoons olive oil
1 teaspoon MasterFoods Freshly Crushed Garlic
1 tablespoon MasterFoods Parsley Flakes
1 tablespoon MasterFoods Sweet Basil Leaves
1 onion (sliced)
plain flour (seasoned with salt and pepper)
30g butter

Method
1. Add extra juice to cold water, and soak cutlets (for a minute or two). Remove cutlets to a shallow dish.

2. Combine lemon juice, olive oil, garlic, parsley, basil and onion slices. Pour over cutlets.

3. Cover, and refrigerate (for at least 3 hours).

4. Drain cutlets well, and toss in seasoned flour.

5. Melt butter in frying pan, add cutlets, and cook over moderate heat (for 2–3 minutes each side).

Serves 4

Blue Eye Cod with Dill Sauce

Ingredients
4 blue eye cod fillets
plain flour
2 eggs (lightly beaten)
125g dry bread crumbs
oil (for shallow frying)

Dill Sauce:
125mL mayonnaise
125mL sour cream
1 tablespoon MasterFoods Dill Leaf Tips
1 tablespoon MasterFoods Parsley Flakes
1 small white onion (finely chopped)
1 teaspoon lemon juice
salt and pepper (to taste)

Method
1. Coat fillets in flour, and then in eggs and breadcrumbs. Heat oil in frying pan.

2. Add fillets, and cook for 2–3 minutes each side (or until cooked through).

3. **Dill Sauce:** Combine all ingredients. Mix well. Chill.

Serves 4

Cod Provençale

Ingredients
2 tablespoons olive oil
30g butter
1 large onion (chopped)
1 teaspoon MasterFoods Freshly Crushed Garlic
2 large tomatoes (peeled and chopped)
¼ teaspoon Master Foods Thyme Leaves
salt and pepper
750g blue eye fillets

Method
1. Heat oil and butter in frying pan, and sauté onion and garlic (until onion is soft).

2. Add tomatoes and thyme, cook for 2–3 minutes, and season with salt and pepper.

3. Add fish to pan, and cover. Simmer for about 20 minutes (or until fish flakes easily with a fork).

Serves 4

Fish in Chilli Sauce

Ingredients
750g blue eye fillets
125g plain flour
85g cornflour
1 egg-white
100mL water
oil for deep frying

Sauce:
1 tablespoon oil
1 tablespoon MasterFoods Freshly Chopped Ginger
1 teaspoon MasterFoods Freshly Crushed Garlic
2 teaspoons MasterFoods Tomato Paste
125mL MasterFoods Sweet Thai Chilli Sauce
2 teaspoons sugar
1 tablespoon MasterFoods Soy Sauce
2 tablespoons dry sherry
2 tablespoons water

Method
1. Cut fillets into 2.5cm-cubes.

2. Sift flour and cornflour into a bowl. Make a well in the centre. add egg-white and water, mix to a smooth batter, and beat well.

3. Heat oil in a pan or wok, dip fish pieces in batter (to coat completely), and drain off excess batter.

4. Lower fish pieces into hot oil, cook for about 5 minutes (until golden brown and cooked through). Drain.

5. **Sauce:** Place all ingredients in a pan or wok. Stir (over medium heat) for 1 minute.

6. Add fish pieces, and toss over high heat (until fish pieces are coated with sauce, and heated through).

Serves 4

Baked Cod Cutlets with Maître d'Hôtel Butter

Ingredients
1 medium onion (finely chopped)
125g MasterFoods Parsley Flakes
125g celery leaves (chopped)
6 blue eye cutlets
1½ teaspoons MasterFoods Madras Curry Powder
salt and pepper (to taste)
3 rashers bacon

Maître d'hôtel Butter:
125g softened butter
2 tablespoons lemon juice
2 teaspoons MasterFoods Parsley Flakes
salt and freshly ground black pepper (to taste)

Method
1. Preheat oven to moderate temperature (180°C).

2. Mix onion, parsley and celery leaves together, and sprinkle onto base of a large, greased, shallow baking dish.

3. On both sides of cutlets, sprinkle the curry powder, pepper and salt.

4. Arrange cutlets on parsley mixture, and place half a rasher of bacon on each. Bake uncovered in a moderately hot oven for 25–30 minutes (or until fish flakes easily when gently pierced).

5. **Maître d'Hôtel Butter:** Blend all ingredients together. Form into a log-shape, and chill.

6. Serve fish with slices of Maître d'Hôtel Butter on top.

Serves 6

BREAK
Yellow-Fin Bream is the marketing name
(Black, Sea, Silver, Surf, Yellow-Fin)

Large head, with steep-profiled snout. Single dorsal fin and long pectoral fin. Bronze-yellow reflections over body; black margin to tail. Fine table fish. Flesh white, with a fine texture and sweet flavour.

Availability: One of the most common of the marine fishes; abundant in creeks, rivers, estuaries, and coastal waters. Generally slightly less than 500g (average), but they can grow to 3–4kg.

Storage: Will have a longer shelf life if bled and gutted immediately after capture. Scale, gill, clean, and trim fins. Best refrigerated whole by wrapping in GLAD Wrap, or stored in airtight GLAD Snap Lock Bags. Refrigerate for 2–3 days (or freeze for up to 6 months).

Preparation: Scale, gill, clean, and trim fins. Completely remove the black lining of the abdominal cavity and also scrape away the white fat along the abdominal wall. Score whole fish before cooking (for even heat penetration).

Cooking: Normally serve one fish per person. Shallow-fry, grill, poach or barbecue. Can be used in mousseline and quenelles. Consider contrasting flavours of capers, citrus, garlic, parsley and ginger: these will marry well with the sweet distinctive taste of bream.

Bream Fillets with Thai Sauce
Ingredients
250mL coconut cream
2 tablespoons Thai red curry paste
juice of 1 lime
1 teaspoon MasterFoods Coriander Leaves
piece lemon grass
1 clove garlic (crushed)
4 bream fillets
2 tablespoons butter
plain flour
MasterFoods Black Peppercorns (freshly ground)
1 teaspoon fish sauce
2 tablespoons lime juice (extra)

Method
1. In a shallow dish combine coconut cream, curry paste, lime juice, coriander, lemon grass and garlic.

2. Add fish and coat well with marinade. Cover, and refrigerate for 3 hours.

3. Heat butter in pan over moderate heat.

4. Remove fish from marinade, drain well, and coat lightly with flour.

5. Cook fillets (until cooked through). Remove and keep warm.

6. Add marinade to pan with pepper, fish sauce and extra lime juice, and heat (to just below boiling). Pour over fish.

7. Remove lemon grass before serving.

Serves 4

Bream Bake
Ingredients
2 tablespoons lemon juice
2 tablespoons water
1 tablespoon MasterFoods Tomato Paste
125mL dry sherry
4 large bream fillets
salt and pepper (to taste)
90g butter
1 teaspoon MasterFoods Freshly Crushed Garlic
250g fresh breadcrumbs
1 tablespoon MasterFoods Parsley Flakes

Method
1. Preheat oven to moderate temperature (180°C).

2. Combine lemon juice, water, tomato paste and sherry. Pour over fillets in a greased casserole dish. Season with salt and pepper.

3. Melt butter, sauté crushed garlic, and combine with breadcrumbs and parsley.

4. Sprinkle crumb topping over fish. Bake in a moderate oven for 25–30 minutes.

Serves 4

Fillet Of Bream with White Sauce and Grapes
Ingredients
4 tablespoons butter
4 bream fillets
125g mushrooms (finely sliced)
2 teaspoons MasterFoods Chopped Chives (Freeze Dried)
24 seedless grapes
1 tablespoon MasterFoods Parsley Flakes
125mL sour cream
125mL mayonnaise

Method
1. Melt butter in frying pan (over moderate heat).

2. Add the fish and cook for about 3 minutes on each side (or until cooked). Remove from pan and keep warm.

3. Add mushrooms and chives to pan, and cook (over low heat) for 1 minute.

4. Add grapes, parsley, sour cream and mayonnaise. Cook whilst stirring (until just heated through). Pour sauce over fish.

Serves 4

Jan's Handy Tip
Place ingredients in a GLAD Oven Bag to keep liquid ingredients near fish and to trap moisture.

Bream with Cucumber

(photographed below)

Ingredients

2 small cucumbers
125g button mushrooms
4 whole bream
salt and pepper
1 tablespoon lemon juice
1 tablespoon sweet chilli sauce
125mL dry white wine
60g butter

Method

1. Preheat oven to moderate temperature (180°C).
2. Thinly slice cucumber and mushrooms, and layer half into a greased casserole dish. Put fish on top, and season with salt and pepper (to taste). Sprinkle combined lemon juice and chilli sauce over dish, and top with remaining cucumber and mushrooms.
3. Pour wine over dish, and dot with 30g butter. Cover and cook in a moderate oven for 30 minutes (or until fish is tender).
4. Remove fish (with cucumber and mushrooms) and keep warm.
5. Drain liquid from pan into a small saucepan, bring to boil, and boil rapidly (adding remaining butter in small pieces).
6. When liquid is reduced to a light glaze, pour over fish.

Serves 4

Baked Fish Parcels

Ingredients

20g butter
1 onion (finely chopped)
1 teaspoon MasterFoods Freshly Crushed Garlic
4 large bream fillets
½ teaspoon MasterFoods Dill Leaf Tips
1 tablespoon MasterFoods Parsley Flakes
2 tablespoons lemon juice
150g mushrooms (sliced)
425g can tomatoes (drained and roughly chopped)
MasterFoods Black Peppercorns (freshly ground, to taste)

Method

1. Preheat oven to moderate temperature (180°C).
2. Heat butter in pan, add onion and garlic, and cook, stirring (until onion is soft). Cool.
3. Place fish onto 4 pieces of GLAD Bake, and spoon onion and remaining ingredients over fish.
4. Fold baking paper around fish, and seal. Place on oven tray.
5. Bake in moderate oven for about 20 minutes (or until fish is cooked through).

Serves 4

Bream with Cucumber

CORAL TROUT

Coral Trout is the marketing name
(Leopard Trout, Lunar Tailed Rock Cod)

A beautiful pink to reddish brown fish with bright blue spots, which tend to fade quickly after capture. One of Australia's premier food fishes, with white, firm, textured flesh and a sweet flavour.

Availability: Found around coral reefs in the tropical waters off Queensland, Northern Territory and Western Australia. Average size is 2kg; however, there are records of over 22kg-individual fish being taken.

Storage: Scale, gill and gut. Wrap whole fish (or fillets) in GLAD Wrap and keep in refrigerator for 2–3 days (or freezer for up to 6 months).

Preparation: Scale, gill and gut whole fish or fillet. Always score whole fish and thick fillets before cooking (for even heat penetration).

Cooking: One average fish (or 2kg of fillets) is sufficient for 2–4 adults. A moist fish lends itself to dry cooking methods, particularly whole-fish baked, steamed, poached or barbecued. Fillets are best grilled, fried, steamed, baked or barbecued. Use only mild sauces, herbs and spices such as parsley, lime, lemon, coriander, cinnamon and chives.

Coral Trout with Mussel Sauce

Ingredients
1 tablespoon butter
1 onion (sliced)
1 leek (sliced)
3 teaspoons MasterFoods Freshly Crushed Garlic
300g mussels
rind of 2 lemons (grated)
70mL white wine
250mL water
100mL cream
small bunch fresh tarragon
4 coral trout fillets

Method
1. Heat butter with sliced onion and leek, and cook over low heat (until vegetables are soft).

2. Add garlic, mussels and grated lemon rind, and cook for a further 2 minutes, increasing the heat.

3. Add wine, cup of water, cream and tarragon, and cook (until liquid is reduced to half). Blend all ingredients in food processor or blender.

4. Grill trout fillets for approximately 4 minutes each side (until cooked), and serve with sauce.

Serves 4

Coral Trout Baked in Paper

Ingredients
4 coral trout fillets
salt and pepper
16 button mushrooms
8 slices lemon
8 shallots (chopped)

Method
1. Preheat oven to moderate heat (180°C).

2. Place trout fillets on 4 pieces of GLAD Bake non-stick paper, and season with salt and pepper.

3. Place 4 mushrooms, 2 slices of lemon and chopped shallots on each fillet. Wrap paper around fillets, and seal well.

4. Bake in preheated moderate oven (for about 20 minutes).

Serves 4

Coral Trout with Chilli and Coriander Pesto

Ingredients

Pesto Sauce:
250g pesto
½ bunch coriander
5 cloves garlic (crushed)
1 jalapeño chilli
1 large Spanish onion
1 chilli
50g walnuts
salt and pepper (to taste)

1 coral trout (about 750g, filletted)
6 tablespoons olive oil
MasterFoods Black Peppercorns (freshly ground)
rock salt
green salad (for serving)

Method
1. Blend all sauce ingredients together (until smooth).

2. Over medium heat, heat a heavy-based frypan. Brush fillets with olive oil, sprinkle with ground pepper and rock salt, and sear for approximately 6 minutes on each side (until golden brown).

3. Serve with pesto sauce and green salad.

Serves 4

Steamed Coral Trout with Ginger, Green Onions and Coriander

Ingredients

750g coral trout (cleaned and gutted)
½ teaspoon salt
4 spring onions (trimmed)
4 slices ginger (unpeeled)
2 tablespoons MasterFoods Soy Sauce
2 tablespoons dry sherry
½ teaspoon sugar
85mL basic fish stock (page 39)
2 tablespoons oil
1 clove garlic (split lengthwise)
65g MasterFoods Coriander Leaves

Method

1. Sprinkle fish with salt. Cut a 5cm-piece from each spring onion at the bulb-end, and cut the green parts lengthwise into very fine long julienne. Set the green parts aside, and place the spring onion bulbs into a heat-proof dish 2.5cm smaller than the steamer to be used. Place fish in the dish, and top with ginger slices.

2. Combine the soy sauce, sherry, sugar, and stock. Spoon it over the fish and marinate for 20 minutes (basting once or twice). When ready to cook, put 8cm of water into a wok fitted with a steamer basket, and bring it to a rolling boil.

3. Place the dish containing the fish into the steamer basket, cover tightly, and steam over high heat for 15–20 minutes (until the fish is just barely opaque through the thickest point). With a knife, pierce the fish along the back at the thickest part, and gently lift the blade (to check for doneness).

4. Just before serving, heat the oil and garlic in a small pan (until very hot). When garlic begins to colour, remove it and discard (keeping the oil).

5. Remove the plate of fish from the steamer. Scatter the coriander and the tangle of green onion tops on the surface, and pour the hot oil over all. Serve immediately.

Serves 4

DHUFISH

**West Australian Dhufish is the marketing name
(WA Pearl Perch, Westralian Jewfish)**

This fish is considered to be one of the finest eating fish in Australia. A white-fleshed, delicate and sweetly flavoured fish with soft texture, medium flake and low- to medium-oil-content.

Availability: Most of the year, with an abundance in summer. Sold mainly in fillets, they are also available whole and in cutlets.

Storage: Scale, gill, gut and thoroughly wash whole fish. Best refrigerated by wrapping in GLAD Wrap or stored in airtight GLAD Snap Lock Bags. Refrigerate for 2–3 days (or freeze for up to 6 months).

Preparation: Very thick fillets should be scored well with a sharp knife (to allow even heat penetration). This is not required if wrapped in foil and baked. Cutlet may be boned (if desired).

Cooking: Gentle cooking without the use of strong flavours is advisable. Pan-fry, lightly steam or grill. An ideal fish cut in raw, thin strips for sashimi. Recommended cooked with a light tempura batter and deep-fried.

Fish Fillets with Artichokes

Ingredients
8 small dhufish fillets
plain flour
2 eggs (beaten)
2 tablespoons milk
400g fresh breadcrumbs
60g butter
2 tablespoons oil

Sauce:
30g butter
1 onion (finely chopped)
350g plain flour
250mL milk
125mL white wine
470g can artichoke hearts (drained and sliced)
125mL cream
2 teaspoons MasterFoods Original Dijon Mustard
1 tablespoon MasterFoods Parsley Flakes
salt and pepper (to taste)

Method
1. Coat fillets with flour (shaking off excess), dip in combined eggs and milk, and coat well with breadcrumbs.
2. Melt butter with oil in large pan, add fish, and fry (until well browned on both sides, and cooked through).
3. **Sauce:** Melt butter, add onion, and sauté (until onion is soft).
4. Over low heat, add flour, and stir (until smooth). Gradually add milk and wine (stirring constantly). Increase heat (to moderate), and stir (until sauce boils and thickens).
5. Add artichokes, and simmer (for 2 minutes). Add cream, mustard, parsley, salt and pepper, and reheat (without boiling).

Serves 4

> ### Jan's Handy Tip
> Keep **Chilli Fish** marinade close to fish and, to prevent unnecessary odours, marinate in a GLAD Oven Bag.

Dhufish with Lemon Sauce

Ingredients
4 dhufish fillets
plain flour
1 egg (lightly beaten)
oil (for shallow frying)

Sauce:
2 tablespoons cornflour
350mL water
1 small chicken cube
125mL lemon juice
1 teaspoon lemon zest
60g brown sugar
2 tablespoons MasterFoods Parsley Flakes
1 tablespoon MasterFoods Chopped Chives
1 teaspoon MasterFoods Thyme Leaves

Method
1. Toss fillets in flour, coat with beaten egg, and then dip in flour again.
2. Heat oil in frying pan and cook fillets for 3–4 minutes on each side (or until cooked through).
3. **Sauce:** Blend cornflour (with a little of the water) in a saucepan.
4. Add remaining water, crumbled stock cube, juice, zest and sugar. Mix well.
5. Cook, stirring over moderate heat (until sauce boils and thickens). Stir in herbs.
6. Pour over fish.

Serves 4

Chilli Fish

Ingredients
750g dhufish fillets
1 teaspoon MasterFoods Freshly Crushed Garlic
1 tablespoon hoisin sauce
1 tablespoon MasterFoods Soy Sauce
65mL MasterFoods Sweet Thai Chilli Sauce
65mL lime juice
1 tablespoon honey

Method
1. Cut fish into 5cm-strips.
2. Combine remaining ingredients and mix well. Add fish and marinate for 30 minutes.
3. Drain fish from marinade. Reserve marinade.
4. Grill fish (until cooked through), brushing occasionally with marinade.

Serves 4

Liz's Bouillabaisse

Ingredients

100g butter
½ bunch celery tops (chopped)
2 large onions (chopped)
2 x 750g cans chopped tomatoes
2 teaspoons MasterFoods Freshly Crushed Garlic
60g MasterFoods Sweet Basil Leaves
60g MasterFoods Thyme Leaves
60g MasterFoods Parsley Flakes
30mL Worcestershire sauce
375mL chicken stock
1 large potato (chopped)
375mL dry white wine
500mL V8 juice (or tomato juice)
12 mussels (scrubbed)
15 medium prawns (deveined and shelled)
8 scallops (shucked)
1 cray tail
125g can crabmeat (or fresh if available)
250g dhufish
250g blue eye cod
crusty bread (for serving)

Method

1. In a large saucepan: melt butter and sauté the celery and onion (until onion is transparent).

2. Add tomatoes, garlic, herbs and Worcestershire sauce. Mix in the chicken stock. Simmer for 2 hours.

3. Add potato. Simmer for a further two hours.

4. Add wine and V8 juice, and simmer for another 2 hours.

5. Allow to cool. Leave in the refrigerator overnight.

6. Before serving, return sauce to heat and, when nicely simmering, add shellfish and fish (one at a time), and allow to simmer (until cooked).

7. Serve with crusty bread.

Note: Fish should be added in order of cooking time. Add longest cooking varieties first and quickest cooking variety last, until all cooked. The order as listed in the Ingredients is the correct order in which to add them.

Serves 8

DORY
(John, Mirror, King, Silver)

Pointed snout, compressed body, elongated spiny dorsal fin. Mainly olive-grey or greenish-silver fish, the John Dory has a large, yellow-outlined, black spot on both sides of its body. An important food-fish with firm-textured, white flesh.

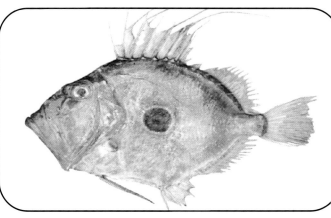

Availability: Trawled in deep waters on the continental shelf of the southern States. Strays as far north as Bundaberg in Queensland. Average size around 1kg. Oreos are similar to Dories and can be used as alternatives.

Storage: Fillets are normally sold with the skin on. Wrap fillets in GLAD Wrap and keep in refrigerator for 2–3 days; will keep frozen for up to 6 months.

Preparation: Only about 25 per cent-recovery rate as the head and gut are large. Normally cooked with skin on. Remove all bones.

Cooking: An average fillet is about 180g, which is enough for a single serve; however, larger fillets are available at your fish market. A moist, low- to medium-oil fish which can be baked, grilled, fried, steamed, poached or barbecued. For baking or steaming use tarragon, dill, parsley, thyme and chives. Stronger flavours (such as chilli, coriander and lime) are better when frying. Dory flavour is delicate; therefore take care not to overpower it with the additives.

Pan Fried John Dory
Ingredients
30g butter
juice of 1 lemon
1 tablespoon sherry
1 tablespoon MasterFoods Parsley Flakes
1 tablespoon MasterFoods Chopped Chives
4 John Dory fillets

Method
1. Melt butter in frying pan, and add lemon juice, sherry, parsley and chives.

2. Add fish, and cook (over fairly hot heat) for 3–4 minutes each side. Serve pan juices over fish.

Serves 4

Mirror Dory with Sauce Véronique
Ingredients
30g butter
1 tablespoon oil
plain flour
500g mirror dory fillets
2 eggs (lightly beaten)
125g dry breadcrumbs
Sauce Véronique:
65mL dry vermouth
250mL dry white wine
125mL water
65mL cream
30g butter
200g white seedless grapes
1 tablespoon water
3 teaspoons cornflour

Method
1. Heat butter and oil in frypan.

2. Coat fillets in flour, then in eggs and breadcrumbs. Add to frypan and cook for 3–4 minutes on each side (or until cooked through).

3. **Sauce:** Combine vermouth, wine and water in a small saucepan, bring to boil and boil uncovered (until reduced by half).

4. Reduce heat, add butter and cream, and stir (without boiling) until butter melts. Add grapes and combined water and cornflour, and stir (until sauce boils and thickens).

Serves 4

Silver Dory with Peppercorn Sauce
Ingredients
plain flour
pepper and salt
4 silver dory fillets
milk
60g butter

Sauce:
30g butter
5cm-piece of green ginger (finely sliced)
3 teaspoons canned green peppercorns
2 tablespoons lemon juice
2 teaspoons lemon rind (grated)
125mL sherry
1 tablespoon brown sugar

Method
1. Season flour with salt and pepper. Dip fillets in milk, and then in flour.

2. Melt butter in frying pan. Add fillets to frypan, and quickly cook 2–3 minutes each side (or until fish flakes when tested with a fork).

3. **Sauce:** Melt butter in a small saucepan, and sauté ginger (for 1 minute).

4. Add remaining ingredients, and bring to boil.

5. Reduce heat and simmer (uncovered) for 10–15 minutes (or until sauce is slightly thickened). Serve with fish.

Serves 4

Silver Dory with Sesame Sauce

(photographed below)

Ingredients

500g silver dory fillets
2 tablespoons lemon juice
30g butter (melted)

Sesame Sauce:

3 tablespoons butter
1 medium onion (chopped)
1 teaspoon MasterFoods Ground Cumin Seeds
1 teaspoon MasterFoods Coriander Leaves
2 tablespoons sweet sherry
3 tablespoons tahini
2 tablespoons peanut butter
1 tablespoon honey
1 tablespoon lemon juice
65mL water

Method

1. Sprinkle lemon juice over fillets, and brush with melted butter.

2. Grill under a hot griller for 2–3 minutes each side (or until cooked through).

3. **Sauce:** Melt butter in a saucepan. Add onion, cumin and coriander, and cook (stirring) for 1 minute.

4. Add remaining ingredients, and stir over moderate heat for about 5 minutes (or until sauce has thickened).

Serves 4

Sautéed Dory Fillets with Blueberries

Ingredients

750g dory fillets
seasoned flour
125g fresh blueberries
1 tablespoon lemon juice
1 teaspoon lemon zest (finely grated)
1 teaspoon sugar
2 tablespoons butter
2 tablespoons MasterFoods Chopped Chives (Freeze Dried)
salt & pepper (to taste)

Method

1. Coat fillets with seasoned flour. In a bowl combine blueberries, lemon juice, rind and sugar, and mix well (until blueberries are slightly softened, yet not squashy).

2. In a frypan: melt butter, and then gently cook fillets for 2–3 minutes on each side. Add blueberry mixture, chives, salt and pepper, and gently heat through.

3. Serve immediately (with extra sauce served in a gravy dish).

Serves 4–6

Jan's Handy Tip

We lunched on both of the above Dory recipes, served with the Mount Pleasant "Lovedale" Hunter Semillon, an Australian classic. The result was pure heaven—fish and wine blended perfectly.

Silver Dory with Sesame Sauce

FLATHEAD

(Dusky, Tiger, Bartailed, Deepwater, Sand, Bluespot, Northern Sand, Rock, Southern, Long-Nosed, Marbled, Mud, Red Spot)

Flattened, depressed head; elongated depressed body; sharp spines on both sides of head. The upper surface of the body is profusely spotted with brown. The pectoral and ventral fins are similarly marked. There are over 30 species of Flathead in Australian waters. A white flesh with a fine- to medium-texture.

Availability: Caught all-year-round, but abundant from October to May. Available as frozen fillets, skin on, and chilled (either filletted or whole).

Storage: Scale, gill and gut. Wrap whole fish or fillets in GLAD Wrap and store in refrigerator for 2–3 days (or up to 6 months in freezer).

Preparation: Scale, gill and gut, but keep skin on. Trim all fins including the 'wing' part of the fillet.

Cooking: Allow 1–2 fillets per serve. Traditional fried fish for 'fish & chips'. Cook in a light batter with salt, tartare sauce or mayonnaise. Try flavouring the flour with curry powder or Cajun spices, or coat fillets with tomato paste, balsamic vinegar and garlic. Scale carefully before cooking (as fine scales will not cook off).

Fillets Of Fish Provençale
Ingredients
4 fillets of flathead
1 large onion (finely sliced)
4 large tomatoes (peeled and sliced)
2 teaspoons MasterFoods Freshly Crushed Garlic
1 tablespoon MasterFoods Parsley Flakes
salt and freshly ground MasterFoods Black Peppercorns
2 large potatoes (very finely sliced)
Parmesan cheese (grated)

Method
1. Place fillets in a greased casserole, cover with the onion slices, and then with the tomato slices. Sprinkle (over each fillet) a little garlic, parsley, salt and pepper.

2. Place pototo slices to completely cover, and sprinkle with Parmesan cheese.

3. Bake at 200°C for 20–30 minutes (or until fish is cooked and potatoes are golden).

Serves 4

Teriyaki Flathead
Ingredients
2 teaspoons MasterFoods Freshly Crushed Garlic
2 teaspoons MasterFoods Freshly Chopped Ginger
2 tablespoons MasterFoods Teriyaki Sauce
1 tablespoon lemon juice
125mL dry white wine
4 flathead fillets
125mL olive oil

Method
1. Combine garlic, ginger, sauce, lemon juice and wine in a shallow dish, and add fillets. Allow to marinate (for 1 hour), turning occasionally.

2. Heat a frying pan (greased with a little oil), and cook fillets, basting with remaining marinade (until fish is cooked).

Serves 4

Oriental Grilled Flathead
Ingredients
2 tablespoons MasterFoods Soy Sauce
12mm piece of green ginger (finely chopped)
1/4 teaspoon MasterFoods Garam Masala
2 tablespoons dry white wine
4 thick flathead fillets

Method
1. Combine soy sauce, ginger, garam masala and wine in a shallow dish, and marinate fish (for an hour), turning once.

2. Line the grill pan with OSO Aluminium Foil, and place fillets in it skin-side-up.

3. Spoon half the marinade over the fish, and grill (at the hottest heat) for 5 minutes.

4. Spoon the remaining marinade over the fish, and continue grilling (until the fish is cooked).

Serves 4

Fish Burgers
Ingredients
750g flathead fillets
60g fresh breadcrumbs
2 tablespoons MasterFoods Parsley Flakes
1 egg (lightly beaten)
2 teaspoons MasterFoods Lemon Pepper Seasoning
plain flour
6 hamburger buns
MasterFoods Lemon Tartare Sauce (for spreading)
lettuce leaves
tomato (sliced)
Spanish onion (sliced)

Method
1. Process fish, breadcrumbs, parsley and egg (until smooth), and stir in lemon pepper seasoning.

2. Divide mixture into 6 portions and shape into a 'hamburger'. Toss 'hamburgers' lightly in flour, and cook in a well-greased frying pan (for about 5 minute on each side).

3. Toast split buns, and spread with tartare sauce.

4. Place salad ingredients on bun, and top with fish burger.

Serves 4

Lemon Crumbed Flathead
(photographed below)

Ingredients
120g fresh breadcrumbs
3 teaspoons lemon rind (grated)
2 teaspoons MasterFoods Madras Curry Powder
1 tablespoon MasterFoods Parsley Flakes
1 tablespoon MasterFoods Dill Leaf Tips
1 teaspoon MasterFoods Ground Turmeric
8 flathead fillets
plain flour
2 eggs (lightly beaten)
oil (for shallow frying)

Cucumber Dressing:
250mL yogurt
2 tablespoons MasterFoods Mint Flakes
1 small cucumber (finely diced)
1 teaspoon MasterFoods Freshly Crushed Garlic
1 teaspoon caster sugar

Method
1. Combine breadcrumbs, lemon rind, curry powder, parsley, dill and tumeric.

2. Toss fish in flour, shake off excess, dip in eggs, and then in breadcrumb mixture. Refrigerate for 30 minutes.

3. Heat oil in frying pan, and cook fish (until cooked through). Serve with cucumber dressing.

4. **Cucumber dressing;** Combine all ingredients and chill.

Serves 4

Baked Whole Flathead with Mussels

Ingredients
3 x 500g flathead (whole)
500g mussels
320mL white wine
250mL basic fish stock (page 39)
2 medium onions (thickly sliced)
2 MasterFoods Bay Leaves
6 whole MasterFoods Black Peppercorns
2 x 425g cans tomatoes
1 tablespoon MasterFoods Sweet Basil Leaves
salt (to taste)
12 black olives

Method
1. Preheat oven (to 180°C).

2. Scale and clean fish (leaving heads on). Wash and scrub mussels (removing beards).

3. Place fish in a large oven-to-table baking dish, combine all ingredients (except mussels and olives), and pour over fish.

4. Place in a preheated oven (at 180°C) for 15 minutes (or until fish begins to flake).

5. Add mussels to dish and cook for another 10 minutes (or until mussels begin to open).

6. Before serving, remove bay leaves and peppercorns. Garnish dish with olives.

Serves 6

> ## Jan's Handy Tip
> Store bay leaves in a GLAD Snap Lock Bag to trap in the flavour.

Lemon Crumbed Flathead

FLOUNDER
(Arrowtooth, Bay, Greenback, New Zealand, Long-snouted, Spotted)

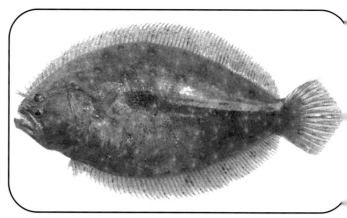

There are reputed to be about 80 species of flat fish in Australian waters. Small head, both eyes on one side of body. A fine-bone structured fish, with white, soft flesh with fine flake and very sweet taste.

Availability: Available all-year-round. Most flounder sold in Australia are imported from New Zealand, where they are caught in commercial quantities.

Storage: Whole fish should be scaled, gilled and gutted. Wrap fillets in GLAD Wrap and keep in refrigerator for 2–3 days. Will keep frozen for up to 6 months.

Preparation: Flounder is often served whole, scaled, gilled and gutted, and can either be boned-out or left with bone in for better presentation. If fish is too large, prepare fillets.

Cooking: Flounder is a wonderful fish to bake whole, as is, or with a stuffing of fresh herbs and lemon zest. A delicately flavoured fish which goes best with dill, chives, lemon, thyme, parsley, tarragon, basil and paprika.

Cantonese-Style Flounder
Ingredients
750g flounder fillets
1 teaspoon MasterFoods Freshly Crushed Garlic
1 teaspoon MasterFoods Freshly Chopped Ginger
2 tablespoons lemon juice
1 tablespoon sherry
2 tablespoons MasterFoods Soy Sauce
1 tablespoon oil
salt and pepper (to taste)

Method
1. Preheat oven to moderate temperature (200°C)
2. Mix together all ingredients (except fish) in a shallow ovenproof dish. Add fish to marinade. Cover and refrigerate (for at least 1 hour).
3. Allow to come back to room temperature before cooking (in a moderate oven) for 20–30 minutes (or until fish is cooked).

Serves 4

Flounder with Sour Cream Sauce
Ingredients
1 tablespoon butter (softened)
65mL lemon juice
1 teaspoon lemon rind (grated)
4 flounder fillets
salt and pepper

Sauce:
50g butter
½ red capsicum (chopped)
1 small onion (finely chopped)
250mL sour cream
2 teaspoons lemon juice
½ teaspoon MasterFoods Worcestershire Sauce
salt and pepper

Method
1. Combine butter, lemon juice and rind. Spread on one side of each fillet. Season with salt and pepper.
2. Place in OSO Aluminium Foil-lined grillpan, and grill with coated side towards grill (until slightly browned). Turn fish and spread other side with butter mixture.
3. Grill until fish flakes when tested with a fork.
4. **Sauce:** Melt butter in saucepan, and add onion and capsicum. Sauté until onion is soft.
5. Add sour cream, lemon juice and Worcestershire sauce, and season (to taste). Bring to boil. Pour over fish before serving.

Serves 4

Flounder with Special Sauce
Ingredients
60g soft breadcrumbs
1 small zucchini (grated)
1 tablespoon MasterFoods Parsley Flakes
2 tablespoons shallots (finely chopped)
30g melted butter
juice of 1 lemon
8 small flounder fillets

Sauce:
2 tablespoons butter
2 tablespoons flour
250mL milk
125mL thickened cream
3 gherkins (finely chopped)
6 black olives (pitted and finely sliced)

Method
1. Preheat oven to moderate temperature (180°C).
2. Mix together breadcrumbs, zucchini, parsley and shallots. Bind together with some of the melted butter and lemon juice.
3. Spread some breadcrumb mixture on each fillet, and roll-up tightly.
4. Place rolls standing up on one end in a shallow, casserole dish lined with GLAD Bake. Sprinkle with remaining lemon juice and butter.
5. Bake in a moderately hot oven for about 15 minutes (or until cooked).
6. Remove fish to a heated serving dish, and keep warm.
7. **Sauce:** Melt butter, add flour, and cook (stirring) for 1 minute. Add milk, and bring to the boil (stirring).
8. Remove from heat and stir in cream, gherkins and olives. Gently reheat. Spoon sauce over fillets.

Serves 4

Flounder with Prawn Sauce

Ingredients
500g flounder fillets
lemon juice
seasoned flour
125g butter

Sauce:
375mL milk
¼ teaspoon MasterFoods Parsley Flakes
1 MasterFoods Bay Leaf
6 MasterFoods Black Peppercorns
1 tablespoon onion (finely chopped)
45g butter
3 tablespoons plain flour
125mL cream
150g cooked prawns

Serves 4

Method
1. Sprinkle fillets with lemon juice, and lightly coat with seasoned flour.
2. Melt butter in frying pan, add fish, and cook (until golden brown and tender).
3. Remove to a serving dish, and keep warm.
4. **Sauce:** Combine milk, parsley, bayleaf, peppercorns and onion in a saucepan, and heat gently for 10 minutes (but do not boil). Remove from heat, and strain.
5. Melt butter in saucepan, add flour, and cook, stirring (over low heat), for 2 minutes. Remove from heat and gradually add warm milk mixture.
6. Return to moderate heat and cook (stirring constantly) until mixture boils and thickens.
7. Add cream and shelled prawns. Heat through. (Do not allow to boil.)
8. Spoon sauce over fish before serving.

GARFISH

(Eastern Sea, Northern, River, Southern, Black-Barred, Long-Beaked, Snub-Nosed, No-Bill, Needle)

Prolongation of the lower jaw forms a beak, usually tipped with bright orange or red. Dorsal and anal fins opposite. Green/silver upper body and silver below.

Availability: Caught all year round but abundant in summer. Normally sold whole; fillets are available on occasions.

Storage: The gut must be removed promptly to avoid staining of the flesh by seagrass. Store with or without head; gutted and scaled. Best refrigerated whole by wrapping in GLAD Wrap or stored in airtight GLAD Snap Lock Bags. Refrigerate for 3–4 days (or freeze for up to 6 months).

Preparation: Normally deep-fried whole. To be different, run a sharp knife down both sides of rib-cage and break backbone at base of tail. Remove the backbone by pulling it towards the head. Push the flesh down with the blunt side of a knife as you do.

Cooking: Cook garfish whole in a deep-fry, or pan-fry. Can be baked, grilled or poached. For something different, fill with favourite stuffing such as prawns, mussels, tomato and rice (or spread with a paste of your favourite herbs).

Chinese Garfish Fillets, Summer Mesclun and Sweet Chilli Sauce

(photographed page 33)

Ingredients
50g Szechwan pepper (crushed)
250g cornflour
1½ teaspoons MasterFoods Chinese Five Spice powder
50g salt
1kg garfish fillets (all bones removed; skin on)
mesclun (to serve)

Chilli Sauce:
3 large red chillies
4 teaspoons MasterFoods Freshly Crushed Garlic
3 tablespoons MasterFoods Coriander Leaves
4 coriander roots
250g sugar
130mL Thai coconut vinegar
130mL water
30mL Thai fish sauce

Method
1. Blend Szechwan pepper, cornflour, five-spice powder and salt together, and sieve. Lightly coat the garfish fillets; then deep-fry (at 180°C) for 1–2 minutes.

2. Chop garlic and coriander roots finely. Boil sugar, Thai vinegar and water together. Remove from heat and add chopped ingredients, garlic, coriander leaves and fish sauce. (This sauce will have a long life if kept in refrigerator.)

3. To serve, place mesclun salad and fish on a serving plate with the sweet chilli sauce (as a dipping sauce) in a small dish on the side.

Serves 6

Whole Garfish

Ingredients
16 whole garfish (cleaned and scaled)
seasoned flour
butter
olive oil
zest and juice of 2 limes
125mL white wine
½ bunch fresh basil (chopped)
½ bunch fresh oregano (chopped)
3 medium tomatoes (diced with no seeds)

Method
1. Preheat oven (to 200°C).

2. Flour garfish. Heat oven-proof frypan or baking tray on medium heat.

3. Place a nob of butter and a splash of olive oil in pan. Cook garfish in pan (until golden brown).

4. Sprinkle zest, juice, wine, herbs and tomatoes over garfish.

5. Cover with OSO Aluminium Foil and place in the preheated oven (at 200°C) for approximately 10 minutes.

Alternative: Bake all ingredients in a GLAD Oven Bag—trap in moisture and keep your oven clean.

Serves 4–6

Crumbed Garfish

Ingredients
12 garfish fillets
125g plain flour
3 eggs (beaten)
60g breadcrumbs
10g mixed dried herbs
3 tablespoons butter

Sauce:
250mL MasterFoods Light Tartare Sauce
juice of 2 lemons
MasterFoods Cracked Black Peppercorns

Method
1. Pass fillets through flour, dip in the beaten eggs, and then dip in a combined breadcrumb and herb mixture.

2. Heat butter in a shallow frypan over medium heat, and add crumbed garfish. Cook until golden brown.

3. Combine tartare sauce, lemon juice and cracked pepper, and serve with garfish.

Serves 4

Chinese Garfish Fillets, Summer Mesclun and Sweet Chilli Sauce

GEMFISH

Gemfish is the marketing name (Hake, King Couta, Kingfish, Silver Kingfish, Southern Kingfish)

A deep-sea fish of the same family as the southern barracouta or snook. Pointed snout, large eyes, long body, forked caudal fin. Silvery-blue in colour. Grow to about 100cm, and provide large fillets with few bones.

Availability: About 90 per cent are caught during the winter months. Very popular as a creamy-pink, moist, firm table-fish, with mild flavour and large flake. Seldom sold as a whole fish; is normally available in both fillets and cutlets (and also smoked).

Storage: Best refrigerated by wrapping in GLAD Wrap, or stored in airtight container. Refrigerate for 2–3 days (or freeze for up to 6 months). Smoked fish should be wrapped in paper or foil. Do not wrap in plastic (as it causes the fish to sweat). Keep refrigerated for 7–10 days.

Preparation: Very thick fillets should be scored well with a sharp knife to allow even heat-penetration. The skin can be left on, or removed. If using cutlets, remove the middle bone and stuff the cavity with your favourite seasoning.

Cooking: Suits all methods of cooking: poaching, frying, grilling, baking or barbecuing. Add your choice of basil, oregano, curry, cumin, tarragon, dill, garlic, soy, mustard, coriander, parsley.

Crumbed Marinaded Gemfish

Ingredients
4 gemfish fillets
70mL lemon juice
2 teaspoons MasterFoods Freshly Crushed Garlic
65g dry breadcrumbs
30g fresh breadcrumbs
200g Parmesan cheese (grated)
2 tablespoons MasterFoods Parsley Flakes
1 teaspoon MasterFoods Cracked Black Peppercorns
1 tablespoon lemon rind (grated)

Method
1. Preheat oven to moderate temperature (180°C).
2. Combine fish, lemon juice and garlic. Cover, and refrigerate for several hours (turning fish occasionally); then drain.
3. Combine breadcrumbs, cheese, parsley, pepper and lemon rind. Mix well. Press mixture evenly over fillets, and place on a sheet of GLAD Bake on an oven tray.
4. Bake in moderately hot oven for about 15 minutes (or until fish is cooked).

Serves 4

Crispy Cutlets

Ingredients
1 tablespoon lemon juice
1 teaspoon MasterFoods Lemon Pepper Seasoning
1 teaspoon MasterFoods Freshly Crushed Garlic
1 tablespoon oil
4 gemfish cutlets
60g fresh breadcrumbs
4 shallots (chopped)
1 teaspoon MasterFoods Original Dijon Mustard
65g cheese (grated)

65g mushrooms (finely chopped)
65g capsicum (finely chopped)
1 egg (beaten)

Method
1. Preheat oven to moderate temperature (180°C).
2. Combine lemon juice, lemon pepper seasoning, garlic and oil. Add cutlets, and marinate (for half an hour).
3. Combine breadcrumbs, shallots, mustard, cheese, mushrooms, capsicum and egg.
4. Divide mixture evenly among cutlets, pressing mixture on firmly.
5. Bake uncovered in moderately hot oven for about 20 minutes (or until cutlets are cooked).

Serves 4

Gemfish with Egg Sauce

Ingredients
4 gemfish fillets
olive oil
lemon juice
salt and freshly ground MasterFoods Black Peppercorns

Sauce:
375mL milk
2 hard-boiled eggs
3 tablespoons butter
3 tablespoons flour
½ teaspoon MasterFoods Horseradish Cream
¼ teaspoon MasterFoods Mustard Powder
salt and pepper
1 tablespoon MasterFoods Chopped Chives (Freeze Dried)

Method
1. Brush fillets with olive oil and lemon juice, and season with salt and pepper.
2. Place under a preheated grill and cook until cooked through (about 8 minutes), turning once.
3. **Sauce:** Blend milk and hard-boiled eggs together (until smooth).
4. Melt butter, stir in flour, and cook over low heat (stirring constantly for 3 minutes).
5. Add milk and egg mixture, horseradish cream, mustard, salt and pepper (to taste). Use a whisk to combine well. Simmer for 8–10 minutes (whisking frequently).
6. Stir in chives, and serve with fish.

Serves 4

Gemfish Curry

(photographed below)

Ingredients

1 tablespoon MasterFoods Madras Mild Curry
1 teaspoon MasterFoods Freshly Crushed Garlic
1 medium onion (chopped)
2 teaspoons lemon juice
250mL plain yogurt
4 gemfish fillets
2 tablespoons olive oil
1 tablespoon MasterFoods Mint Flakes

Method

1. Preheat oven to moderate temperature (200°C).

2. Place curry paste, garlic, onion, lemon juice and yogurt in a food processor, and process (until smooth).

3. Place fillets in a shallow ovenproof dish.

4. Heat oil in a large frying pan, add blended mixture, and stir over medium heat (until it comes to the simmer). Continue to cook (stirring) for 2 minutes.

5. Pour over fish and bake in the moderate preheated oven for 20 minutes (or until fish is cooked). Sprinkle mint over dish.

Serves 4

Gemfish Potato Casserole

Ingredients

6 medium potatoes
30g butter
85mL hot milk
300mL sour cream
1 small onion (finely chopped)
6 gemfish fillets
65g dry breadcrumbs
2 tablespoons cheese (grated)
MasterFoods Ground Paprika

Method

1. Preheat oven to moderate temperature (200°C).

2. Boil potatoes. When cooked, mash with butter and hot milk. Spread potato into the bottom of a large, shallow, greased casserole dish.

3. Spread one third of the sour cream over the potatoes, and spoon chopped onion over.

4. Arrange fish on top. Sprinkle with combined breadcrumbs and cheese. Spread remaining sour cream over crumb mixture, and sprinkle with paprika.

5. Bake in the moderately hot preheated oven for 30 minutes.

Serves 6

Gemfish Potato Casserole

JEWFISH

Black Jewfish is the marketing name (Spotted, Mulloway, Butterfish, Soapies, Teraglin, Trag, Silver)

Long, moderately compressed body, with distinct and separate dorsal fins. The flesh is pale-pink, with a large- to medium-flake, and a firm texture. Mild flavours make this an excellent table fish.

Availability: Most of the year. Sold both whole and in cutlet form, with smaller fish sold filletted.

Storage: Scale, gill, gut and thoroughly wash whole fish. Best refrigerated by wrapping in GLAD Wrap or stored in airtight GLAD Snap Lock Bags. Refrigerate for 2–3 days (or freeze for up to 6 months).

Preparation: Very thick fillets should be scored well with a sharp knife to allow even heat penetration. This is not required if wrapped in foil and baked. Cutlet may be boned if desired.

Cooking: As it is a slightly dry fish the moist cooking methods are most appropriate. An ideal fish to stuff and to serve with sauce. Seasonings such as curry powder, garlic, chilli, cumin, coriander, tarragon and parsley are tasty additions.

Pan-Fried Fish with Mushroom Sauce
Ingredients
4 jewfish cutlets
plain flour
30g butter

Sauce:
30g butter
4 bacon rashers (chopped)
1 medium onion (chopped)
75g baby mushrooms (sliced)
½ red capsicum (chopped)
85mL thickened cream
2 green shallots (chopped)
2 teaspoons cornflour
1 tablespoon water

Method
1. Toss fish in flour. Shake off excess flour.

2. Heat butter in a large frying pan, add fish, and cook (over medium heat) for about 4 minutes on each side (or until fish is tender). Serve with sauce.

3. **Sauce:** Melt butter in a saucepan, and add bacon and onion. Stir constantly over medium heat for about 2 minutes (or until onion is soft). Add mushrooms and capsicum, and cook for a further minute.

4. Add cream, shallots and cornflour (blended with water). Cook, stirring constantly (until sauce boils and thickens).

Serves 4

Spanish-Style Fish Cutlets
(photographed page 37)
Ingredients
4 jewfish cutlets
olive oil
1 tablespoon MasterFoods Parsley Flakes
3 teaspoons MasterFoods Freshly Crushed Garlic
30g almonds (slivered)
1 tablespoon shallots (chopped)
½ teaspoon MasterFoods Ground Paprika
½ teaspoon lemon rind (grated)
425g can tomatoes (drained and roughly chopped)

Method
1. Preheat oven to moderate temperature (180°C).

2. Arrange fish in a shallow ovenproof dish which has been lightly brushed with olive oil. Brush the top of each cutlet with olive oil.

3. Combine parsley, garlic, almonds, shallots, paprika, lemon rind and 1½ tablespoons olive oil. Spoon over fish, and press down well.

4. Bake fish in a moderate oven for 10 minutes.

5. Pour the tomatoes around the fish, and cook for a further 10 minutes (or until fish is cooked).

Serves 4

Jewfish Steaks with Mango Sauce
Ingredients
1 teaspoon sambal oelek (or hot chilli sauce)
3 tablespoons oil
3 tablespoons dry white wine
3 tablespoons lemon juice
4 jewfish steaks

Sauce:
425g can mangoes
2 tablespoons mango chutney
1 teaspoon MasterFoods Soy Sauce
1 teaspoon lemon juice
½ teaspoon sambal oelek (or hot chilli sauce)

Method
1. Combine sambal oelek (or hot chilli sauce), oil, wine and lemon juice, and brush over steaks.

2. Cook under a moderate grill for 5–6 minutes on each side (or until cooked through).

3. **Sauce:** Drain mangoes, reserving 65mL syrup. Blend mangoes and syrup with remaining ingredients.

4. Place sauce in a small saucepan and stir over low heat (until heated through).

Serves 4

Spanish-Style Fish Cutlets

KINGFISH
(Yellowtail, Samson, Black)

Different varieties of Kingfish are found below the Tropic of Capricorn around Australia. They grow to a large size and are popular both as a sporting fish and as a table fish.

Availability: Smaller fish: mainly caught in summer months of December–February. Medium to larger fish are caught mainly in late spring. Offered whole, and as fillets or cutlets.

Storage: Cut fish into fillets or cutlets before storing. Best refrigerated by wrapping in GLAD Wrap or stored in airtight container. Refrigerate for 2–3 days (or freeze for up to 6 months).

Preparation: Kingfish has a soft, mild flavour, is medium in oil-content with a medium-dry moisture-content and medium-to-firm texture. Prepare as fillets or cutlets.

Cooking: Most suitable for grilling, baking, barbecuing and frying. Makes great sashimi. Cook with strong flavours such as Cajun spices, chilli, soy, ginger, lemon and garlic. As fish is fairly dry it is sometimes prudent to marinate prior to cooking.

Fish Steaks in a Parcel
Ingredients
2 tablespoons butter
6 shallots (chopped)
2 teaspoons MasterFoods Freshly Crushed Garlic
125g mushrooms (sliced)
450g can tomatoes (drained and roughly chopped)
½ teaspoon sugar
12 black olives (pitted and sliced)
375g raw prawns (peeled and deveined)
4 kingfish steaks
salt and freshly ground MasterFoods Black Peppercorns
1 tablespoon lemon juice

Method
1. Preheat oven to moderate temperature (200°C).

2. Heat butter in a frying pan, and sauté shallots and garlic.

3. Add mushrooms, tomatoes, sugar, olives and prawns. Simmer for 2–3 minutes, stirring continuously. Cool.

4. Place fish on four pieces of GLAD Bake non-stick baking paper. Sprinkle with salt, pepper and lemon juice. Spoon topping over, fold paper over fish, seal, and place on baking tray.

5. Bake in the preheated moderately hot oven (for about 25–30 minutes).

Note: Using GLAD Bake to parcel fish not only keeps fish tender, but also prevents fish from sticking to the baking tray.

Serves 4

Jan's Handy Tip
Kingfish has a strong, distinct and pleasing flavour. It has only a few bones (which are easily removed), and is adaptable to all kinds of appetising approaches. Experience the majesty of the ocean reef in all its succulent splendour.

Kingfish Steaks with Eggplant and Tomato Sauce
Ingredients
750g eggplant
1½ teaspoon salt
1 capsicum (green)
1 spring onion
1 tablespoon olive oil
750g kingfish steaks (skin removed, about 2cm-thick)
salt and pepper to taste
lemon juice
plain flour
250mL tomato sauce
85mL dry vermouth
1 teaspoon MasterFoods Freshly Crushed Garlic
1 MasterFoods Bay Leaf
¼ teaspoon MasterFoods Thyme Leaves

Method
1. Peel the eggplant and cut into 1.5cm-cubes (making about 4–5 cups). Place in a colander, pour salt over, toss, and set aside (for about 20–30 minutes).

2. Halve the capsicum, remove stem and seeds and cut into 5mm-lengthwise slices. Peel, halve and cut the onion into 5mm-lengthwise slices. Cook onion and capsicum slowly with the oil (in a 25cm frypan) for several minutes (until vegetables are tender).

3. Drain the salted eggplant, spread on several thicknesses of paper towels, and pat dry.

4. Remove the cooked onion and capsicum to a side-dish, leaving the oil in the frypan. (If necessary, add more oil to liberally cover frypan base.)

5. Raise heat to moderately high. When hot, add the dried eggplant. Toss frequently for several minutes (until eggplant is moderately browned).

6. Season fish lightly with salt, pepper and lemon juice. Just before sautéing, press steaks in flour and shake off excess.

7. Pour 2mm-layer of oil into a heavy based frypan and heat. When very hot, sauté the steaks for 4–5 minutes each side. Fish is cooked when a fork flakes flesh easily.

8. Arrange steaks on serving platter.

9. Add the cooked onions and capsicum to the sautéed eggplant. Add the tomato sauce, vermouth, garlic and herbs. Boil slowly for several minutes (to make a thick sauce).

10. Serve with sauce poured over fish.

Serves 4

Kingfish with Mustard and Capers (Microwave Recipe)

(photographed below)

Ingredients

4 tablespoons butter (softened)
1 tablespoon MasterFoods Original Dijon Mustard
1 tablespoon capers (chopped)
½ teaspoon salt
½ teaspoon MasterFoods Cracked Black Peppercorns
4 x kingfish cutlets (each 185–250g)
¼ teaspoon MasterFoods Ground Paprika

Method

1. Mix butter and mustard in a small bowl (until smooth). To this add capers, salt and pepper, and mix well. Spread equal amounts evenly over each fillet. Sprinkle paprika on top.

2. Place fillets in a large microwave safe dish and cover with GLAD Wrap (folding back one edge to allow steam to escape).

3. Cook on High until opaque throughout (about 5–7 minutes, depending on thickness of fillets).

4. Let stand for at least 2 minutes (covered) before serving.

5. Serve with a selection of steamed vegetables.

Serves 4

Spicy Kingfish Steaks

Ingredients

4 kingfish steaks
1 small onion (chopped)
125mL red wine
1 tablespoon MasterFoods Tomato Paste
6 MasterFoods Black Peppercorns
½ teaspoon MasterFoods Horseradish Cream
½ teaspoon MasterFoods Mustard Powder
1 tablespoon MasterFoods Sweet Basil Leaves

Method

1. Put fish in shallow dish. Combine remaining ingredients, and pour over fish.

2. Stand for 30 minutes. Drain, and reserve marinade.

3. Cook under hot grill for about 6 minutes each side, basting with reserved marinade.

Serves 4

Basic Fish Stock

Ingredients

1kg fish heads and bones
9 cups water
juice of 1 lemon
2 onions (sliced)
1 MasterFoods bay leaf
1 teaspoon MasterFoods parsley flakes
½ teaspoon MasterFoods thyme
leafy top from 1 celery stalk
1 teaspoon salt

Method

1. Rinse fish-bits and place in saucepan with remaining ingredients. Bring to a simmer and brew uncovered for about 20 minutes. When ready, strain through a sieve and allow to cool, then skim off top. Ideal stored in GLAD Ice-Cube Bags, in freezer, until required.

Kingfish with Mustard and Capers (Microwave Recipe)

MACKEREL

(Spanish, Grey, School, Spotted, Indo-Pacific, Wahoo, Chub, Frigate, Leadenall, Jack, Horse, Scad, Cowan Young, Doggie, Shark, Snook, Salmon Mackerel, Tiger)

Bluish-green-to-black above; silver belly. Long, fusiform body. Different species in the family can grow from 50cm to 180cm.

Availability: All year round with seasonal peaks in each State or Territory. Normally sold whole, in fillets or in cutlets.

Storage: Best made into 'meal-packs', then refrigerated by wrapping in GLAD Wrap or stored in airtight GLAD Snap Lock Bags. Refrigerate for 2–3 days or freeze for up to 6 months.

Preparation: Very thick fillets should be scored well with a sharp knife to allow even heat-penetration. The skin (which is thin and edible) can be left on, or removed. If using cutlets: remove the middle bone and stuff the cavity with your favourite seasoning.

Cooking: Can be marinated, poached, fried, grilled, barbecued or smoked. Take care not to overcook. High oiliness: often requires the balance of an acid to enhance the richness. Do this by baking with vinegar and vegetables.

Mackerel Pizzaiola

Ingredients
1½ tablespoons olive oil
1 large onion (thinly sliced)
2 teaspoons MasterFoods Freshly Crushed Garlic
450g can tomatoes (peeled, seeded and chopped with liquid)
60mL water
60g minced MasterFoods Parsley Flakes
½ teaspoon salt
¼ teaspoon MasterFoods Black Peppercorns (freshly ground)
1 tablespoon olive oil (extra)
3 x medium-sized mackerel (heads removed, split, rinsed and dried)
60g breadcrumbs (fresh, soft)
65g Parmesan cheese (freshly grated)

Method
1. Preheat oven (to 230°C). In a medium frypan, heat olive oil. Add onion and garlic, and cook for 1 minute. Add tomatoes, water, parsley, salt and pepper, and cook for 3 minutes.
2. Grease a large baking dish with additional olive oil. Place fish (skin side-down) in dish. Pour tomato mixture over fish. Bake for 15–25 minutes (baking time depending on the thickness of fish).
3. When fish is cooked, sprinkle breadcrumbs and cheese over top, then place under griller until brown (1–2 minutes).

Serves 6

Jan's Handy Tip

En Papillote: This is a French term meaning 'to cook in paper'. Wrap your choice of fish and ingredients in GLAD Bake Paper, and bake. Fish will not dry out, and is cooked when the paper 'puffs up'. Serve by opening the parcel just before taking to the table—the aroma is delicious.

Corn and Pepper Mackerel Boats

Ingredients
4 x mackerel fillets (each 185–250g)
½ teaspoon salt
¼ teaspoon MasterFoods Cracked Black Peppercorns
2 x 270g cans corn kernels
1 capsicum (medium red, finely diced)
1 teaspoon MasterFoods Freshly Crushed Garlic
4 tablespoons butter (melted)

Method
1. Preheat oven to 230°C.
2. Lie fish flat on 4 pieces of GLAD Bake (each about 30cm x 40cm). Season with salt and pepper. Sprinkle equal amounts of corn, capsicum and garlic over each fillet, and drizzle one tablespoon melted butter (over each).
3. Fold top of paper over bottom, and crimp edges tightly to seal. Arrange packets on a baking plate in a single layer. Bake 10–12 minutes (or until paper is puffed and fish flakes easily).

Serves 4

Baked Mackerel with Fennel and Prosciutto

Ingredients
3 tablespoons olive oil
2 teaspoons MasterFoods Freshly Crushed Garlic
fennel leaves (about 250g)
60g breadcrumbs (fresh, soft)
3 slices prosciutto (slivered)
½ teaspoon salt
¼ teaspoon MasterFoods Black Peppercorns (freshly ground)
2 x 750g mackerel (whole)

Method
1. Preheat oven to 230°C.
2. Heat olive oil in a medium fry pan. Add garlic and fennel, and cook for 1 minute. Add breadcrumbs and prosciutto. Toss to coat with oil, add salt and pepper, and mix well.
3. Cut to deep scores on both sides of each fish. Stuff scores with as much bread mixture as possible. Place fish in a large, well-buttered baking dish. Sprinkle remaining bread mixture over fish.
4. Bake 15–20 minutes (baking time depends on thickness of fish). When cooking is complete, place fish under griller (just long enough to brown topping).

Serves 4–6

Grilled Mackerel

Ingredients

65mL mayonnaise
2 teaspoons MasterFoods Original Dijon Mustard
½ teaspoon salt
½ teaspoon MasterFoods Cracked Black Peppercorns
4 x mackerel fillets (each 185–250g)

Method

1. Heat griller. Combine all ingredients (except fish) in a small bowl. Arrange fillets on a lightly oiled grilling tray, and spread equal amounts of mixture evenly over each.

2. Grill 10–15cm away from heat (without turning) for 6–8 minutes (or until golden brown on top and opaque throughout). Serve immediately.

Serves 4

Jan's Handy Tip

Mackerel is high in omega–3–fatty acids—ideal for those on a cholesterol-lowering diet. Lowering blood cholesterol levels has been shown to decrease heart attacks and strokes.

Fish in a Parcel

(photographed below)

Ingredients

4 mackerel cutlets
freshly ground MasterFoods Black Peppercorns
1 tablespoon lemon juice
65g tasty cheese (grated)
4 spring onions (chopped)
1 medium cucumber (sliced)

Method

1. Preheat oven to moderate temperature (180°C).

2. Place each cutlet on a piece of greased, heavy-duty OSO Aluminium Foil. Season with pepper and lemon juice.

3. Divide grated cheese among cutlets. Sprinkle with spring onions, and top each cutlet with cucumber slices (about 4–6 slices on each cutlet).

4. Wrap OSO Aluminium Foil around cutlets and seal. Place on oven tray and bake in a preheated, moderately hot oven (for 20–25 minutes).

Serves 4

Fish in a Parcel

MULLET
Mullet is the marketing name

(Yellow-tail, Sand, Fan-tail, Flat-Tail, Jumping, Blue-Tailed, Diamond scale, Sea, Tiger, Bully, Poddy, Mangrove, Hardgut, Striped, Grey, Yellow Eye)

Small mouth; blunt snout. Commonly bluish above, with silver belly. Elongated cylindrical body with pectoral fins placed high on body. Reputed to be the favourite food of the Ancient Romans who paid high prices for them.

Availability: Most of year with larger catches in Autumn and early winter. Sold both whole and filletted.

Storage: Scale, gill, clean and trim fins. Completely remove the black lining of the abdominal cavity, and also scrape away the white fat along the abdominal wall. Best refrigerated by wrapping in GLAD Wrap or stored in airtight GLAD Snap Lock Bags. Refrigerate for 2–3 days (or freeze for up to 3 months).

Preparation: Flavour and oil-content varies according to species. Use whole or filletted, or butterflied by removing head and slitting belly from head to tail. Remove insides and flatten opened fish on a board, flesh-side down. Press firmly along the backbone, then turn over and pull out backbone and any other bones.

Cooking: Most species have a very rich oil-content, and therefore are best baked, barbecued, shallow-fried or grilled. Great if smoked.

Baked Mullet with Tomatoes
Ingredients
4 small mullet
30g butter
1 large onion (chopped)
1 teaspoon MasterFoods Freshly Crushed Garlic
450g can tomato pieces
1 tablespoon MasterFoods Tomato Paste
2 tablespoons MasterFoods Parsley Flakes
1 tablespoon lemon juice
2 teaspoons lemon rind (grated)
6 pimento stuffed olives (sliced)

Method
1. Place fish in a greased baking dish.

2. Melt butter in saucepan, add onion and garlic, and sauté (until onion is soft). Remove from heat and add remaining ingredients. Stir well to combine, and pour sauce over fish. Cover.

3. Bake in moderate slow oven for 20–25 minutes.

Serves 4

Grilled Mullet
Ingredients
4 x mullet fillets (each about 185g)
65mL red vinegar
4 teaspoons olive oil
½ teaspoon salt
¼ teaspoon MasterFoods Cracked Black Peppercorns
¼ teaspoon MasterFoods Ground Paprika

Method
1. Preheat griller. Place fish on a lightly oiled grilling plate, and spoon about 1 tablespoon vinegar over each fillet. Drizzle each with 1 teaspoon olive oil, and season with salt and pepper.

2. Grill 10–15cm from heat for about 8 minutes (until lightly browned). Remove from griller, dust with paprika, and serve immediately.

Serves 4

Mullet Mediterranean
Ingredients
3 teaspoons butter
2 tomatoes (peeled and sliced)
1 small capsicum (cored, seeded and sliced)
125g button mushrooms (sliced)
salt
MasterFoods Black Peppercorns (freshly ground)
4 x mullet (scaled and cleaned)
65mL red wine
2 tablespoons MasterFoods Chopped Chives

Method
1. Preheat temperature to moderate temperature (180°C).

2. Melt 2 tablespoons butter in a shallow casserole dish. Add vegetables, and cook gently for 5 minutes (stirring occasionally). Season with salt and pepper.

3. Place mullet side-by-side on top of vegetables, and pour wine over top. Sprinkle with chives, and dot with remaining butter.

4. Cover and bake in a preheated moderate oven (180°C) for 20–30 minutes (or until fish flakes easily when tested with a sharp knife).

Serves 4

Jan's Handy Tip
To remove scales easily, rub fish with vinegar first—you will find that the scales come off easily.

Try draining fried fish on stale pieces of bread instead of kitchen paper. You will find that the bread absorbs the run-off fat easily.

Jan's Handy Tip
Those prejudiced against Mullet would be surprised to learn how many people in the fish industry prefer it to other varieties. Not everybody likes an oily flavour; this can be overcome by skinning the fish. Mullet is usually such good value for money that it deserves another chance. A great wine to drink with Mullet is the Mount Pleasant Chardonnay, an example of the Hunter's finest.

Greek-Style Mullet with Olives and Feta Cheese

(photographed below)

Ingredients

4 x mullet fillets (each 125–185g)
65mL olive oil
125g Feta cheese
250g black olives (pitted, coarsely chopped)
2 teaspoons fresh lemon juice
½ teaspoon MasterFoods Cracked Black Peppercorns

Method

1. Preheat oven (to 220°C). Place each fillet in centre of a piece of OSO Aluminium Foil (each about 30 x 40cm). Drizzle 1 tablespoon olive oil over each. Crumble equal amounts of cheese over each fillet, and scatter olives on top. Sprinkle each fillet with a small amount of lemon juice, and season with pepper.

2. Fold top of foil over bottom. Crimp edges tightly to seal. Arrange packets on a baking tray in a single layer. Bake for 10–12 minutes (until foil is puffed and fish is opaque throughout).

Serves 4

Curried Coconut Mullet

Ingredients

750g mullet fillets
6 tablespoons coconut (desiccated)
1½ tablespoons MasterFoods Madras Curry Powder
2 eggs (lightly beaten)
2 tablespoons margarine
3 bananas (peeled, cut lengthways)
2 lemons (cut in wedges)
250g natural yogurt

Method

1. Rinse fillets and wipe-over with paper towel. Mix coconut and curry powder on a plate. Dip fillets in egg, and then coat with coconut mixture.

2. Heat margarine in a pan, and fry fish fillets for 2–3 minutes each side (until fish flakes). Be careful not to allow coconut to burn. Remove and keep warm.

3. Add banana halves to pan, and cook gently (until just tender). Serve fish with banana, lemon wedges and yogurt.

Serves 6

Greek Style Mullet, with Olives and Feta Cheese

ORANGE ROUGHY

Orange Roughy is the marketing name (Sea Perch, Deep-Sea Perch, Red Roughy)

Please note that Orange Roughy is not a member of the perch family despite its previously being known as 'Sea Perch'. An ugly fish which belies its delightful taste.

Availability: Mainly caught from June to August. Normally available only in chilled or frozen skinless fillets. Not sold with the skin on, because the black lining under the skin can cause severe diarrhoea.

Storage: Best refrigerated by wrapping fillets in GLAD Wrap or stored in airtight GLAD Snap Lock Bags. Refrigerate for 2–3 days (or freeze for up to 3 months).

Preparation: Frying in a herb-crumb mixture will be more suitable than a standard batter. However, a tempura beer batter will not overpower the subtle flavour of the fish.

Cooking: Can be baked, grilled, poached, steamed or deep-fried. Boneless flesh and mild flavour make this fish one of Australia's favourites.

Orange Roughy Parcels

Ingredients
1kg orange roughy fillets (cut into 6 serving pieces)
6 red capsicum rings
6 large mushrooms (sliced thin)
3 tablespoons MasterFoods Parsley Flakes
¼ teaspoon MasterFoods Ground Nutmeg
¼ teaspoon dried MasterFoods Tarragon Leaves
2 tablespoons extra-virgin olive oil
½ teaspoon salt

Method
1. Preheat oven (to 220°C). Cut six pieces of GLAD Bake (non-stick baking paper) into rectangles (each 8cm longer than each piece of orange roughy). Arrange a piece of orange roughy on the side of the paper on top of a red capsicum ring. Arrange a sliced mushroom on each piece of fish. Sprinkle with parsley, nutmeg, and tarragon. Brush with oil, then sprinkle with salt.

2. Fold the sides (and then the ends) of the paper envelope around the fish. Arrange the fish packages on a baking tray. Bake the packages for 6–8 minutes (or until the fish is cooked). The paper will brown lightly when done.

3. Place each package on a plate, and serve it hot. Allow each guest to open their own package.

Serve 6

Crumbed Orange Roughy

Ingredients
250g savoury biscuit crumbs (crushed)
200g tasty cheese (grated)
4 orange roughy fillets
MasterFoods Light Tartare Sauce

Method
1. Combine crushed biscuits and cheese.

2. Coat fillets with tartare sauce, and then with biscuit crumbs (pressing on firmly).

3. Place fish in a shallow baking dish lined with a sheet of GLAD Bake.

4. Cook in a hot oven for 15–20 minutes (or until fish is tender).

Serves 4

Orange Grilled Fish

Ingredients
1 tablespoon MasterFoods Soy Sauce
1 tablespoon orange juice
1 tablespoon orange rind (grated)
1 teaspoon sesame oil
2 tablespoons honey
500g orange roughy fillets

Method
1. In a small saucepan, combine all ingredients (except fish).

2. Heat over a low heat (until honey has melted).

3. Place a sheet of OSO Aluminium Foil on the grill tray, place fillets under grill, and cook (at medium heat).

4. Baste fish with marinade. Cook for approximately 8–10 minutes.

Serves 4

Jan's Handy Tip
A delightful-tasting fish like Orange Roughy demands a crisp, chilled white wine. My suggestion here is a McWilliams Mount Pleasant Semillon Blanc.

Poached Orange Roughy on Wild Rice

Ingredients

250mL water
2 tablespoons lemon juice
2 MasterFoods Sqeeze-On Chicken Stocks
125g shallots (sliced diagonally)
¼ teaspoon MasterFoods Thyme Leaves
¼ teaspoon MasterFoods Ground White Pepper
125g carrots (thinly sliced diagonally)
500g orange roughy fillets
250g wild rice (prepared according to packet directions)
MasterFoods Ground Paprika (for garnish)

Serves 4

Method

1. Combine the water, lemon juice, stock cubes, shallots, thyme and pepper in a deep frypan. Bring liquid to boil. Cover, and simmer for 5 minutes. Add carrot, and let simmer for an extra 4 minutes.

2. Lay the fillets in the liquid without crowding. Cover, and simmer for about 10 minutes (until fish is opaque and flakes easily).

3. Divide the rice between individual plates. Arrange one fillet and some of the vegetable-mix on the rice. Check if mixture is too thin. If so, remove all fish and vegetables from the pan, and boil remaining liquid (to reduce slightly). Pour liquid over the fish and rice, and garnish with paprika.

PERCH—FRESHWATER

(Golden, Murray Cod, Silver, European Carp, Redfin, Yellowbelly)

The edible characteristics of the fresh-water finfish listed vary from Murray Cod to the introduced European Carp. Availability of most wild fresh-water finfish has declined over the years.

Availability: Different species are caught all year round, mainly by anglers. The golden perch is prized in Chinese cooking circles for presentation as a steamed finfish.

Storage: Normally sold in whole form: scale, gill and gut. Wrap whole fish in GLAD Wrap and keep in refrigerator for 2–3 days. Will keep frozen for up to 6 months.

Preparation: Make sure you score whole fish well and skin fillets. Always ask for European Carp that have been purged (allowed to swim in clean, fresh water) for about a week.

Cooking: The majority of these species are suitable for baking, frying, grilling, barbecuing or poaching. Many species of perch have thick white fillets, making them ideal for casseroles, soups, chowders and bouillabaisse. As stated earlier, Golden Perch is particularly good if steamed with Asian flavours, such as ginger, chilli, coriander, soy and garlic.

Pan-fried Perch Fillets with Creamy Sauce

Ingredients
6 perch fillets
flour
2 eggs (lightly beaten)
2 tablespoons milk
125g dry breadcrumbs
1 tablespoon Parmesan cheese (grated)
olive oil (for shallow frying)

Sauce:
30g butter
1 small onion (finely chopped)
1 teaspoon MasterFoods Freshly Crushed Garlic
250mL thickened cream
3 tablespoons MasterFoods Tomato Paste
65g pimiento-stuffed olives (chopped)
MasterFoods Cracked Black Peppercorns and salt (to taste)

Method
1. Toss fillets in flour, shaking off excess. Dip into combined egg and milk, then into combined breadcrumbs and Parmesan cheese. Cover, and refrigerate (for 30 minutes).

2. Heat oil in frying pan, and cook fillets for about 4 minutes each side (or until cooked through). Remove from pan, and keep warm.

3. **Sauce:** In a saucepan, melt butter, and sauté onion and garlic for 2–3 minutes.

4. Add remaining ingredients, stirring constantly (until heated through). Pour over fish.

Serves 6

Perch Fillets with Sesame Sauce

Ingredients
6 perch fillets
plain flour
2 eggs (lightly beaten)
2 tablespoons milk
125g dried breadcrumbs
oil (for shallow frying)

Sauce:
65g butter
65g onion (very finely chopped)
1 teaspoon MasterFoods Freshly Crushed Garlic
½ teaspoon salt
65g plain flour
125g tahini
375mL orange juice
250mL water
1 tablespoon MasterFoods Soy Sauce
1 teaspoon honey

Method
1. Toss fillets in flour, shaking off excess. Dip into combined egg and milk, and then into breadcrumbs.

2. Heat oil in frying pan, and cook fillets.

3. **Sauce:** Melt butter in saucepan. Add onion, garlic and salt, and cook (stirring) over low heat (until onion is soft).

4. Stir in flour, and cook (stirring continuously) for five minutes.

5. Add tahini, and continue to cook (stirring) over lowest heat for another minute. Add orange juice, water, soy sauce and honey.

6. Simmer gently on lowest heat for 10 minutes.

Serves 6

Jan's Handy Tip
When boiling fish, cook in a minimum volume of water (and do not overcook).

When frying fish, try adding a teaspoon of vinegar to the batter, and use water instead of milk.

Add a dessert spoon of olive oil to a beaten egg when crumbing fish or cutlets—it will make crumbs stick more firmly.

Perch Rolls with Tomato Basil Sauce

Ingredients

1 zucchini
1 carrot
1 stick celery
4 perch fillets
toothpicks
pepper and salt
1 tablespoon lemon juice

Sauce:

25g butter
1 medium onion (finely chopped)
1 teaspoon MasterFoods Freshly Crushed Garlic
125mL dry white wine
4 large tomatoes (peeled, seeded and chopped)
1 tablespoon MasterFoods Tomato Paste
salt and pepper
65g MasterFoods Sweet Basil Leaves

Method

1. Preheat oven (to 180°C).
2. Cut vegetables into 10cm-thin strips. Place fillets skin side-up, and season with pepper and salt. Divide vegetable strips amongst fillets, and roll up around vegetables. Secure with toothpicks.
3. Place fish rolls in baking dish, spoon lemon juice over, cover, and bake in a moderately hot oven for 20 minutes (or until cooked through).
4. **Sauce:** Melt butter in a saucepan, add onions and garlic, and cook, stirring (until onions are soft).
5. Add wine, tomatoes, tomato paste, salt and pepper to taste. Bring to a boil, reduce heat, and simmer (until sauce is slightly thickened).
6. Add basil, and stir well. Spoon sauce over fish rolls.

Serves 4

REDFISH
(Nannygai, Red Snapper)

The head, back and fins are red with the sides being a lighter silvery-red. A common fish caught by anglers, it has very large eyes and a single dorsal fin. Caught up to 45cm in length.

Availability: Most of the year but more abundant during spring. Sold both whole and in fillet form.

Storage: Scale, gill, gut and thoroughly wash whole fish. Best refrigerated by wrapping in GLAD Wrap or stored in airtight GLAD Snap Lock Bags. Refrigerate for 2–3 days, or freeze for up to 6 months. Frames and heads are good for finfish stock.

Preparation: As the scales are very tightly knit it is best to fillet and skin whole fish. Best cooked as fillets only; whole fish cooking is not recommended.

Cooking: An excellent method of cooking Redfish is Cajun-style, using selected spices for 'blackened finfish'. Ideal fish for baking, frying and grilling. Suggested seasonings are parsley, lemon, lime, orange (rind & juice), mild mustard, wine, coriander, thyme, dill and mint.

Devilled Fish Fillets
Ingredients
500g redfish fillets
1 tablespoon MasterFoods Horseradish Cream
1 tablespoon MasterFoods Original Dijon Mustard
2 tablespoons tomato sauce
1 teaspoon MasterFoods Worcestershire Sauce
1 teaspoon butter

Method
1. Place fish fillets on greased GLAD Foil on the grill tray. Grill on one side, and turn.

2. Coat each fillet with a mixture of the horseradish, mustard, tomato sauce, Worcestershire sauce and butter.

3. Grill until fish flakes when tested with a fork.

Serves 4

Crème Fraîche
Ingredients
1 litre whipping cream
125mL buttermilk

Method
1. Bring the cream and buttermilk to room temperature, and mix thoroughly. Allow to sit in a warm place (20–25°C) for about 24 hours (or until thick).

2. Refrigerate until ready to serve.

Jan's Handy Tip
The Bight redfish is much larger than the standard redfish, but is equally flavoursome and versatile. Both are quite inexpensive, make excellent eating, and are available as flake-sized finfish or skinless fillets.

They are highly regarded as a major ingredient in fishcakes, quenelles, fish balls, croquettes or gefilte finfish. Because the flesh has good gelling characteristics, very little binder need be added. Redfish are ideal for large-scale catering.

Baked Redfish with Marinated Roast Capsicum
Marinated Roast Capsicum:
3 large red capsicums (cut into 5cm-strips)
125mL extra-virgin olive oil
1 tablespoon MasterFoods Sweet Basil Leaves
1 tablespoon MasterFoods Ground Oregano Leaves
6 teaspoons MasterFoods Freshly Crushed Garlic
½ teaspoon salt
¼ teaspoon freshly ground MasterFoods Black Peppercorns
6 anchovy fillets (or to taste)

3 large tomatoes (halved horizontally)
2 tablespoons extra-virgin olive oil
65g seasoned bread crumbs
1kg redfish fillets 9cut into 6 serving pieces0
200mL dry white wine

Method
1. **Marinated Roast Capsicum:** Grill, capsicum skin side-up, until charred (about 5–7 minutes).

2. Place them into a GLAD Oven bag and seal it shut. When cool, remove skins.

3. Place into a shallow bowl. Pour the olive oil over them, and sprinkle with basil, oregano, garlic, salt, and pepper. Cover with GLAD Wrap, and refrigerate overnight.

4. Before cooking fish, remove capsicum from refrigerator (to warm to room temperature), and arrange anchovy strips decoratively over capsicums. Preheat oven (to 200°C) and line a baking tray with GLAD Bake.

5. Brush tomato halves with the 2 tablespoons of oil, and sprinkle with bread crumbs. Arrange on the paper-lined baking tray.

6. Place the fillets in a large baking dish (lined with GLAD Bake), and sprinkle with wine. Put both the tomatoes and the fish in the oven; and bake fish for 6–8 minutes (tomatoes for 10 minutes). Fish should flake easily when tested. Transfer fish pieces (with a slotted spoon) to individual plates, and add a tomato half to each plate. Serve hot with roast capsicum.

Serves 6

Jan's Handy Tip
As a couple of the Redfish recipes on this page are rather spicy, may I suggest that a fine McWilliams Eden Valley Show Rhine Riesling would be the perfect accompaniment?

Blackened Redfish with Crème Fraîche

Ingredients

125g unsalted butter
125mL freshly squeezed lemon juice
¼ teaspoon each salt, MasterFoods Ground Cayenne
  Pepper, MasterFoods Garlic Powder, and
  MasterFoods Onion Powder
½ teaspoon dried MasterFoods Thyme Leaves
1kg redfish fillets
1 recipe Crème Fraîche (see recipe page 48)

Method

1. Melt butter in a small saucepan over low heat. Stir in lemon juice, salt, cayenne, garlic powder, onion powder, and thyme. Pour the seasoned butter into a shallow dish.

2. Heat a large, heavy frying pan over high heat. Roll the redfish in the seasoned butter, and fry it quickly, turning it once (for about 2 minutes on each side). The redfish will char on the outside and be tender on the inside. With a spatula, transfer the fish to a heated platter.

3. Place the fish on individual plates and serve it hot with a dollop of crème fraîche.

Note: This dish may also be prepared using prepared blackening spices in place of the above seasonings.

Serves 6

SHARK

(Black Tip, Gummy, Whiskery, School, Angel, Saw, Dog, Dusky)

Shark fillets are commonly sold as 'boneless fillets' or 'flake' in Australia. The skeleton of shark is made of cartilage (not bone as in other fishes). Shark is especially safe for children as there is no chance of swallowing bones.

Availability: All of the year. Sold only as skinless fillets or shark fins. Some shark may have an ammoniacal odour after being stored for a few days. Simply soak in fresh water with lemon juice or vinegar to eliminate this.

Storage: Best refrigerated by wrapping in GLAD Wrap or stored in airtight container. Refrigerate for 2–3 days (or freeze for up to 6 months).

Preparation: Very thick fillets should be scored well with a sharp knife to allow even heat-penetration. Ensure that the skin has been removed prior to cooking, for if it is left on it will shrink and tear the flesh.

Cooking: Suits all methods of cooking, most commonly for 'fish & chips'. Be careful not to undercook as thick fillets tend to look cooked on the outside yet remain almost raw on the inside. Excellent for soups, especially Asian-style 'shark-fin soup'.

Shark Provençale (Microwave)

Ingredients

2 tablespoons olive oil (divided)
500g shark fillets
1 ripe tomato
2 shallots or 1 small yellow onion (peeled and minced)
2 teaspoons MasterFoods Freshly Crushed Garlic
2 teaspoons capers (drained)
½ teaspoons MasterFoods Thyme Leaves
¼ teaspoon salt
¼ teaspoon MasterFoods Cracked Black Peppercorns
2 tablespoons MasterFoods Parsley Flakes

Method

1. Place one tablespoon of olive oil in a microwave-safe baking dish. Coat fillets with oil, and arrange in spokes (with thick parts toward the outside and thin portions toward the centre of the dish).

2. Slice tomato in half around the middle, and squeeze gently (to remove seeds and juice). Chop finely. Combine with remaining olive oil, shallots, garlic, capers, thyme leaves, salt, pepper and parsley. Sprinkle over fish.

3. Cover and cook on medium (50%) power for 10–12 minutes (turning fish once halfway through cooking). Fish is done when it is firm to the touch. Allow to stand for 1 minute.

4. Divide fish into serving pieces. Serve with bread or rice.

Serves 4

Barbecued Ginger Shark

Ingredients

3 tablespoons lemon juice
2 tablespoons honey
1 tablespoon MasterFoods Freshly Chopped Ginger
1 tablespoon MasterFoods Soy Sauce
½ teaspoon MasterFoods Chinese Five Spice
500g shark steaks
freshly ground MasterFoods Black Peppercorns (to taste)

Method

1. Combine lemon juice, honey, ginger, soy sauce and five-spice powder in a shallow dish. Coat both sides of fish with mixture and marinate for 30–35 minutes.

2. Drain fish and reserve marinade. Barbecue over medium-low heat for 6 minutes per side, basting frequently. Turn and cook for 5–6 minutes on the other side. Season with pepper, and serve.

3. Discard marinade. Do not allow flames to flare up and scorch the fish. The honey in the marinade will burn if exposed to direct flames.

Serves 4

Shark Teriyaki Barbecue

Ingredients

125mL low-sodium soy sauce
3 tablespoons lemon juice
3 tablespoons sherry or mirin*
1 green onion (finely chopped)
1 tablespoon MasterFoods Freshly Chopped Ginger
1 teaspoon sugar
1 teaspoon MasterFoods Freshly Crushed Garlic
olive oil (for brushing)
500g shark steaks (about 2cm-thick)

Method

1. Combine all ingredients (except fish and olive oil) in a ceramic baking dish. Make sure sugar dissolves. Add fish and turn to coat both sides. Cover and refrigerate for 2–3 hours (or until ready to cook).

2. When ready to cook, preheat barbecue and brush lightly with a coating of olive oil. Drain fish and place each piece of fish on the grill.

3. Baste frequently and cook for 2–3 minutes. Give each fillet a quarter-turn without flipping it. (The quarter-turn gives the fillets an attractive diamond pattern from the grill.) Cook 2 minutes longer.

4. Turn fillets over, baste, and cook for 4 minutes on the second side (for medium-rare) or 5 minutes (for medium). Allow a few minutes longer for extremely thick pieces of fish (but do not overcook).

*Note: Mirin is sweetened saké wine.

Serves 2–4

Barbecued Shark and Vegetables with Orange Vinaigrette

(photographed below)

Ingredients

1kg fresh shark steaks (cut into chunks about 2.5cm-thick)
2 red or yellow capsicums (pierced once with a knife)
12 small red-skinned potatoes (washed)
orange vinaigrette (recipe follows)
3 zucchini (ends trimmed)
1 head radicchio (red chicory)

Method

1. Cut the shark into 6 even pieces. Set aside.

2. Heat a barbecue (until coals are medium-hot). Pierce capsicums with a knife and place on the hottest part of the grill. The skin should blister and char slightly after 12 minutes. Place in an airtight GLAD Snap Lock Bag. Allow to steam and cool. When cool enough to handle, peel away the skin and discard it.

3. If desired, thread all the potatoes on metal skewers. Place them over the hottest part of the fire. Cook for 25–30 minutes (turning occasionally, and basting with the orange vinaigrette).

4. Add zucchini, and cook (until slightly blackened, but tender). Baste occasionally with orange vinaigrette. (Zucchini will require about 8–10 minutes total cooking time.)

5. Add the shark steaks, and cook (for 6 minutes per side). Baste occasionally with orange vinaigrette. Slice radicchio in half lengthwise, and add to grill. Baste with vinaigrette. Cook for 4–5 minutes, until leaves are wilted and slightly charred. Remove all vegetables and fish from grill. Keep warm.

6. Transfer remaining orange vinaigrette to a microwave-safe container. Cook on high (100%) power for 2 minutes, stirring occasionally (until mixture boils). Drizzle over hot vegetables and fish, and serve.

Serves 6

Orange Vinaigrette

Ingredients

2 tablespoons olive oil
1 teaspoon MasterFoods Freshly Chopped Ginger
1 tablespoon MasterFoods Soy Sauce
1 teaspoon orange rind (freshly grated)
250mL orange juice (freshly squeezed)
2 tablespoons vinegar (such as raspberry, balsamic or white wine)
pinch MasterFoods Ground Cayenne Pepper
1 teaspoon MasterFoods Dry Mustard

Method

1. Combine all ingredients. Blend well. Transfer to a container with an airtight lid.

2. Dressing can be made up to one week in advance.

Makes 1¼ cups

Barbecued Shark and Vegetables with Orange Vinaigrette

SNAPPER

Snapper is the marketing name (Cockney, Pinkies, Red Bream, Squire, Schnapper)

Snapper have a number of names which vary according to growth, age and where caught. Small immature snapper are called squire. As they mature they develop the characteristic hump on the head.

Availability: Most of year but more abundant in winter. Available whole, and in both fillet and cutlet form. Heads and frames are ideal for use in finfish stews and stocks.

Storage: Scale, gill and clean. Best refrigerated by wrapping in GLAD Wrap or stored in airtight GLAD Snap Lock Bags. Refrigerate for 2–3 days or freeze for up to 6 months.

Preparation: Whole fish should be scored a few times diagonally on both sides. Very thick fillets should be scored well with a sharp knife to allow even heat-penetration. Cutlet may be boned if desired.

Cooking: Can be steamed, poached, smoked, baked, fried, grilled or barbecued; also can be used for sashimi. Because of its taste and texture, snapper suits most flavourings. The head is most sought-after for Indian curries.

Baked Snapper Spanish Style

Ingredients
1 x whole snapper 2–2.5kg (cleaned, scaled, head & tail intact)
½ teaspoon salt
¼ teaspoon MasterFoods Cracked Black Peppercorns
1 small onion (thinly sliced)
2 tablespoons olive oil
1 teaspoon MasterFoods Freshly Crushed Garlic
4 fresh tomatoes (peeled, seeded & diced)
½ teaspoon lime zest (grated)
¼ teaspoon MasterFoods Chilli Powder
1 tablespoon lemon juice
1 tablespoon lime juice
65g MasterFoods Coriander Leaves

Method
1. Preheat oven to 220°C).

2. Place fish in a 23 x 35cm-baking dish, and season with salt and pepper. Place in the preheated oven.

3. In a medium frypan, cook onion in olive oil over medium-high heat until translucent (about 2 minutes). Add garlic and cook for 1 minute longer. Stir in tomatoes, lime zest and chilli powder. Increase heat to high and cook until sauce thickens (about 2 minutes).

4. Pour tomato mixture over and around the fish, and cover loosely with OSO Aluminium Foil. Bake for 20–30 minutes (or until fish is opaque next to the bone).

5. When cooked, transfer fish to a large serving platter. Sprinkle with lemon and lime juices, and add the coriander over the top. Serve immediately.

Serves 4

Creole Bouillabaisse

Ingredients
Spice Mixture:
2 teaspoons parsley (very finely chopped)
2 MasterFoods Bay Leaves (finely crushed)
1 teaspoon MasterFoods Freshly Crushed Garlic
½ teaspoon salt
¾ teaspoon MasterFoods Thyme Leaves
½ teaspoon MasterFoods Allspice
⅛ teaspoon MasterFoods Freshly Ground Black Pepper

2 tablespoons olive oil
500g snapper fillets
500g redfish fillets
1 large onion (chopped)
250mL white wine
3 large tomatoes (peeled and thickly sliced)
6 lemon slices
250mL hot basic fish stock (page 39)
salt and pepper to taste
dash of MasterFoods Ground Cayenne Pepper
pinch MasterFoods Saffron
6 slices buttered toast

Method
1. Combine spice mixture, and rub into fish fillets.

2. Heat olive oil in a large saucepan (or Dutch oven), and add fish and onion.

3. Cover and cook over low heat for 10 minutes (turning fillets once). Remove fillets from saucepan (and keep warm).

4. Add to saucepan (stirring well) the wine, tomato slices, lemon slices, stock, pepper, salt and cayenne. Simmer for 25–30 minutes (or until liquid is reduced to half).

5. Take 6 tablespoons of the cooking liquid, and blend with the saffron.

6. Place fish back in saucepan, and cook for a further 5 minutes.

7. Pour saffron mixture over fillets. Remove fillets from sauce, and place on toast. Pour sauce over. Serve at once.

Serves 6

Jan's Handy Tip
Dining on the Creole Bouillabaisse recipe above is a delight not to be missed. To further enhance the experience, and to bring out the full flavour of the fish and spices, may I suggest that you serve a new wine from Mount Pleasant, a superb Verdelho?

Jamaican Snapper

Ingredients

1 tablespoon olive oil
4 snapper steaks
10 shallots (chopped)
2 large ripe tomatoes (peeled and chopped)
1 red capsicum (seeded and chopped)
65mL white wine vinegar
½ teaspoon MasterFoods Thyme Leaves
1 tablespoon honey
salt and MasterFoods Black Peppercorns (freshly ground)

Method

1. Heat oil in frying pan. Add steaks, and brown quickly on both sides (on high heat).

2. Add shallots, tomatoes and capsicum. Cover and simmer (for 5 minutes).

3. Add remaining ingredients, bring back to boil, cover, and simmer (for further 15 minutes).

Serves 4

Baked Snapper Niçoise

(photographed below)

Ingredients

1 tablespoon olive oil
3 teaspoons MasterFoods Freshly Crushed Garlic
2 ripe tomatoes (chopped)
1 small onion (finely chopped)
65g capsicum (finely chopped)
65g black olives (pitted and finely sliced)
¼ teaspoon MasterFoods Thyme Leaves
½ teaspoon MasterFoods Tarragon Leaves
375mL dry white wine
4 snapper steaks

Method

1. Preheat oven to moderate temperature (180°C).

2. Heat oil in frying pan and sauté garlic, tomatoes and onion (until soft).

3. Add capsicum, olives, thyme, tarragon and wine. Cook, uncovered (for 5 minutes) over a moderate heat.

4. Place steaks in a greased, shallow, ovenproof dish. Pour sauce over steaks.

5. Cover and cook in the preheated moderate oven for 20 minutes (or until steaks are cooked through).

Serves 4

Baked Snapper Niçoise

TROUT— RAINBOW

Trout is the marketing name (Brown, Ocean)

Trout are not indigenous to Australia. European Brown Trout and Californian Rainbow Trout have been introduced into many streams, lakes and rivers. Trout fishing is extremely popular with recreational anglers. The flesh is soft, white-to-pink, and moist. The flavour is mild.

Availability: Most of the year from trout farms. Usually sold whole; either fresh or smoked. Can occasionally be purchased as fillets.

Storage: Best refrigerated by wrapping in GLAD Wrap or stored in airtight container. Refrigerate for 2–3 days (or freeze for up to 6 months). Smoked fish should be wrapped in paper or foil; do not wrap in plastic as it causes the fish to sweat. Keep refrigerated for 7–10 days. Frozen smoked trout can become salty.

Preparation: Clean, gut and wash. Leave whole (with or without head). Smoked trout is eaten as is, with skin removed, and further cooking is not required.

Cooking: Can be steamed, poached, smoked, baked, grilled or barbecued. Nuts are suitable accompaniments, particularly almonds. Skin the trout after cooking: it's much easier.

Trout with Capsicum
Ingredients
2 tablespoons olive oil
3 teaspoons MasterFoods Freshly Crushed Garlic
½ medium yellow capsicum (cored and sliced)
½ medium red capsicum (cored and sliced)
½ medium green capsicum (cored and sliced)
½ teaspoon MasterFoods Ground Cumin Seeds
1 teaspoon MasterFoods Ground Coriander Seeds
pinch MasterFoods Ground Cloves
salt and MasterFoods Cracked Black Peppercorns
4 large trout fillets

Method
1. Heat half the olive oil in a large frying pan, add the garlic, and sauté until soft and fragrant (about 1 minute).

2. Add the capsicum, and sauté over medium heat (stirring occasionally) until they begin to soften (3–5 minutes). Stir in the cumin, coriander, cloves, salt and pepper. Transfer to a bowl and set aside.

3. Add the remaining olive oil to the pan, and fry the trout fillets (skin-side down) for 3–4 minutes. Turn the fillets, and spoon the capsicum mixture over them.

4. Cover the pan and cook over medium-low heat until the trout is opaque through the thickest part (6–8 minutes longer).

5. Transfer the trout fillets and capsicum garnish to warmed dinner plates, and serve.

Serves 4

Trout Almondine
Ingredients
½ cup almonds (slivered)
2 tablespoons butter
2 tablespoons vegetable oil
125g flour
½ teaspoon salt
¼ teaspoon MasterFoods Cracked Black Peppercorns
4 small whole trout (cleaned and washed; heads and tails intact)
125mL dry white wine

Method
1. In a large frypan, cook almonds in butter and oil over medium heat (stirring often) until lightly browned (3–5 minutes). Remove pan from heat. Remove almonds with a slotted spoon, and set aside. Reserve remaining butter and oil.

2. In a shallow dish, combine flour, salt, and pepper. Dredge trout in seasoned flour to coat. Shake off excess.

3. Cook trout in butter and oil in a frypan (over medium-high heat) turning once, until browned on both sides and opaque near bone (about 7 minutes). Remove to a platter, and cover (to keep warm). Return almonds to skillet, add wine, and raise heat to high. Bring to a boil, pour over fish, and serve at once.

Serves 4

Chillied Trout
Ingredients
1 tablespoon tomato paste
2 teaspoons MasterFoods Ground Chillies
1 tablespoon olive oil
1 teaspoon fresh lemon juice
½ teaspoon salt
6 whole trout (each about 250g; cleaned and washed)

Method
1. Preheat broiler. In a small bowl, combine tomato paste, chilli powder, olive oil, lemon juice, and salt. Stir to blend well.

2. Lie fish out on a work surface. Use fingers to rub each side with about 1 teaspoonful of chilli paste (or to taste).

3. Place fish on a well-oiled grilling plate. Grill about 10cm from heat (about 5 minutes per side) until skin is dark amber and until flesh springs back slightly when pressed at its thickest part.

Serves 4

Grilled Trout Calypso

(photographed below)

Ingredients

4 trout (each about 250g; boned and butterflied)
65mL fresh lime juice
1 tablespoon butter (melted)
½ teaspoon MasterFoods Ground Cumin Seeds
½ teaspoon salt
¼ teaspoon MasterFoods Ground Cayenne Pepper

Method

1. Preheat griller. On a lightly oiled grilling pan, arrange trout (skin-side down) so that they are not touching each other. Spoon about 1 tablespoon of lime juice over each fish. Drizzle each with one teaspoon butter, and season with cumin, salt, and cayenne.

2. Grill (10–15cm from heat) for 6–8 minutes without turning, until lightly browned outside and opaque throughout.

Serves 4

Jan's Handy Tip

Trout is a well-known European species. Now Australian fisheries are producing excellent fresh-water and salt-water varieties. Discover a 'pot-of-gold', with the lovely eating qualities and deep, pink flesh of the rainbow trout.

Whole Steamed Trout Stuffed with Crab

Ingredients

30g fresh bread crumbs
250g crabmeat
2 teaspoons MasterFoods Marjoram Leaves
1 teaspoon salt
½ teaspoon MasterFoods Freshly Ground Black Pepper
2 tablespoons butter (melted)
4 whole trout (each about 250g; cleaned; head and tail intact)

Method

1. In a small bowl, combine bread crumbs, crab, marjoram, ½ teaspoon salt, and ¼ teaspoon pepper. Add butter, and toss lightly to mix.

2. Season inside cavity of trout with remaining salt and pepper. Loosely fill with crab stuffing, and secure with toothpicks.

3. Place trout flat on a steaming rack set over simmering water. Steam (covered) until fish is firm when pressed in centre (about 10 minutes). Remove toothpicks and serve at once.

Serves 4

Grilled Trout Calypso

TUNA
(Yellowfin, Southern Bluefin, Big Eye, Skipjack, Striped, Bonito, Northern)

A great deal of tuna is canned. However the tuna is considered very valuable in the Japanese market as the main fish desired for sushi and sashimi.

Availability: All year with the winter catch considered to be the most valuable. Available whole only from major fish distributors, when it is normally supplied in fillets, steaks, cutlets and trunks.

Storage: It is essential that tuna be stunned, bled and processed immediately on capture to obtain flesh of sashimi quality. Wrap well-bled fish in GLAD Wrap and store in refrigerator for up to 3 days. Can be frozen for about 3 months.

Preparation: Ideal as cutlets and steaks. Slice thinly and serve raw with Japanese warsabi (mustard) and soy.

Cooking: Can be steamed, poached, smoked, baked, grilled or barbecued. Also used for sashimi. Goes well with intense flavours such as charred capsicum, eggplant, balsamic vinegar, roasted garlic, wasabi, soy and ginger. Wrap in OSO Aluminium Foil, coat with favourite herbs, and bake. A word of warning: do not overcook as this may cause the flesh to fall apart.

Oriental Tuna Cutlets
Ingredients
125mL orange juice
1 tablespoon lime juice
65mL MasterFoods Soy Sauce
1 tablespoon hoisin sauce
1 teaspoon MasterFoods Freshly Crushed Garlic
4 tuna cutlets

Method
1. Combine juices, sauces and garlic in a shallow dish. Place cutlets in marinade, cover, and refrigerate for at least 4 hours.
2. Remove from marinade, and drain well. Grill or pan-fry cutlets, basting often with marinade.

Serves 4

Fish Cutlets with Pineapple and Gherkin Salsa
Ingredients
4 tuna cutlets
salt and MasterFoods Cracked Black Pepper
1 small red onion (finely chopped)
2 teaspoons MasterFoods Freshly Crushed Garlic
125g tomato (peeled and chopped)
juice of 1 lemon
125g chopped capsicum
½ fresh pineapple (skinned, cored and chopped)
2 tablespoons cider vinegar
2 teaspoons caster sugar

Method
1. Sprinkle cutlets with salt and freshly ground black pepper. Grill or pan-fry (until cooked through).
2. Mix together the remaining ingredients and spoon over fish.

Serves 4

Pan Fried Tuna with Chilli Sauce
Ingredients
4 tuna cutlets
salt and MasterFoods Cracked Black Pepper
30g butter
125mL dry white wine
125mL cream
1 teaspoon cornflour
1 tablespoon water
1 tablespoon MasterFoods Parsley Flakes
1 tablespoon MasterFoods Sweet Basil Leaves
1 teaspoon sambal oelek (or hot chilli sauce)

Method
1. Season cutlets with salt and pepper.
2. Melt butter in frying pan. Cook cutlets over moderate heat for 3–4 minutes each side.
3. Remove from pan and keep warm. Add wine, cream and cornflour (blended with water), bring to boil and simmer for 1 minute. Add herbs and sambal oelek, simmer (for 1 minute), pour over fish, and serve.

Serves 4

Tangy Tuna Steaks
Ingredients
2 tuna steaks
65mL tomato chutney
1 tablespoon white wine vinegar
2 tablespoons lemon juice
dash Tabasco
1 tablespoon oil
¼ teaspoon MasterFoods Dry Mustard
125mL MasterFoods Light Tartare Sauce
2 teaspoons lemon juice (extra)

Method
1. Place fish steaks in a single layer in a shallow dish.
2. Combine remaining ingredients (except tartare sauce and extra lemon juice). Pour mixture over fish, and let stand for 30 minutes (turning once).
3. Remove fish, and reserve sauce for basting. Place fish steaks on greased foil in the grill pan. Grill (under a medium grill) for 5–8 minutes.
4. Baste generously with sauce, turn, and cook for a further 5 minutes. Spread with combined tartare sauce and extra lemon juice. Cook a further 5 minutes.

Serves 4

Tuna Steaks with White Wine and Asparagus

Ingredients

4 x tuna steaks (each about 150g; cut 2.5cm-thick)
½ teaspoon salt
¼ teaspoon MasterFoods Cracked Black Peppercorns
4 tablespoons butter (melted)
20 asparagus spears (trimmed about 12cm-long)
⅓ each red, yellow and green capsicum (cut into thin
  strips)
65mL white wine

Serves 4

Method

1. Preheat oven (to 215°C). Set out 4 equal pieces of GLAD Bake (each about 30 x 40cm), and place steaks in centre.
2. Season with salt and pepper. Pour one tablespoon butter over each steak.
3. Top with five asparagus spears and spread equal amounts of capsicum strips over each steak. Sprinkle each steak with one tablespoon of white wine.
4. Fold top of paper to bottom and crimp edges tightly to seal. Place on a baking tray in a single layer. Bake for 15–20 minutes (until paper is puffed and steaks are cooked through).

WHITING
(King George, School, Red Spot, Trumpeter, Sand, Yellowfin, Golden-lined, South Australian, Grass, Silver, Spotted)

Whiting are available all-year-round with different species being more plentiful at different times.

A delicate-flavoured moist fish of medium texture and low oil-content.

Availability: Small species sold in whole form. Larger species (such as King George and Sand Whiting) sold in frozen or chilled fillets.

Storage: Scale, gill and clean. Best refrigerated by wrapping in GLAD Wrap or stored in airtight container. Refrigerate for 3–4 days (or freeze for up to 6 months).

Preparation: Scale, gill and clean. Head may be removed or left on. Smaller fish are cooked whole; larger specimens either whole or in fillets (as desired).

Cooking: Frying is the most common means of cooking. However, whiting may be steamed, baked, barbecued and grilled. As it has a fine, moist texture it is best, when frying, to coat fish in a protective coating of flour, a crumb-mixture or light batter. Because of the fine flavour whiting cooks best with mild seasonings, used sparingly.

Whiting Provençale
Ingredients
8 whiting fillets
500mL water
3 MasterFoods Black Peppercorns
1 onion (sliced)
2 lemon slices
pinch MasterFoods Thyme Leaves
2 MasterFoods Bay Leaves

Sauce:
4 tablespoons butter
100g mushrooms (sliced)
4 shallots (chopped)
4 tablespoons flour
4 tablespoons white wine
2 tomatoes (peeled, seeded and chopped)
salt and pepper
1 tablespoon Parmesan cheese

Method
1. Place fish in a large frying pan, add water, peppercorns, onion, lemon slices, thyme and bay leaves, bring to simmering point, cover, and simmer gently for about 15 minutes (or until cooked).

2. Remove fish to an ovenproof dish, and keep warm. Strain frying-pan liquid for use in sauce.

3. **Sauce:** Melt butter in saucepan and sauté the mushrooms and shallots for 2 minutes.

4. Add flour, stir over low heat for a minute, add the strained liquid from the fish, and the wine. Stir until boiling, add tomatoes, and salt and pepper (to taste).

5. Simmer (over very low heat) for 3–4 minutes. Pour sauce over fish, sprinkle with Parmesan cheese, and brown under hot grill.

Serves 6–8

Whiting with Warm Tartare Sauce
Ingredients
500g whiting fillets
plain flour
2 eggs (lightly beaten)
125g dry breadcrumbs
oil (for shallow frying)

Warm Tartare Sauce:
50g butter
2 tablespoons plain flour
2 tablespoons dry white wine
125mL water
1 MasterFoods Squeeze-On Chicken Stock
300mL thickened cream
2 gherkins (chopped)
1 tablespoon capers (rinsed and chopped)
1 tablespoon MasterFoods Parsley Flakes
4 shallots (chopped)

Method
1. Coat fillets in flour, then in egg and breadcrumbs. Heat oil in frying pan.

2. Add fillets and cook 2–3 minutes each side (or until cooked through).

3. **Sauce:** Heat butter in small saucepan, add flour, and cook (stirring, over low heat) for 1 minute.

4. Gradually stir in combined wine, water and crumbled stock cube. Stir until sauce boils and thickens.

5. Remove sauce from heat and whisk in cream, gherkins, capers, parsley and shallots.

6. Return to heat and gently warm through. Do not allow to boil.

Serves 4

Jan's Handy Tip
Stocks and sauces can be frozen in GLAD Ice Cube Bags for easy portions, when required.

When frying fish, it's best to sprinkle a little curry powder in the pan before fish. This will stop the smell and improve the flavour.

To stop fish breaking up in the pan, try salting it first and leaving it for a few hours before cooking.

Whiting and Asparagus

Ingredients

- whiting fish fillets
- tablespoons lemon juice
- 40g can green asparagus spears
- 0g breadcrumbs (fresh)
- alt and pepper
- egg (beaten)
- shallots (finely chopped)

auce:

- 0g butter
- tablespoon plain flour
- 25mL milk
- 5mL asparagus liquid
- 5mL cream
- tablespoons MasterFoods Parsley Flakes
- 0g tasty cheese (grated)

erves 4

Method

1. Preheat oven to moderate temperature (180°C).
2. Sprinkle fish fillets with lemon juice. Leave to stand for 10 minutes.
3. Drain asparagus well, reserving 65mL liquid. Mash, drain off excess liquid, and reserve this also.
4. Combine asparagus with breadcrumbs, season with salt and pepper, add beaten egg and shallots. Mix well.
5. Prepare 4 greased squares of OSO Aluminium Foil, and place one fillet on each (thus using 4 of the 8 fillets). Spread each fillet with asparagus mixture to cover. Top each with a second fillet.
6. Wrap foil around fillets, and seal. Bake in moderate oven (180°C) for 20–25 minutes (or until fish is cooked). Remove from foil, and keep warm.
7. **Sauce:** Melt butter in a saucepan, add flour, and stir (for 1 minute). Gradually add milk, reserved asparagus liquid and cream, stirring constantly (until sauce boils and thickens).
8. Stir in parsley and grated cheese. Pour sauce over fish.

Shellfish and Crustacean Recipes

ABALONE

(Blacklip, Greenlip, Roe's, Brownlip, Mutton Fish, Tiger, Paua)

A single ear-shaped shell, lined with mother-of-pearl. Blacklip has a red shell with black frill across foot; greenlip has a red shell streaked with green across foot. The so-called Marine Opal is cut from the New Zealand paua shell. Abalone has a cream-coloured flesh with a mild flavour.

Availability: Caught all year. Is available live, frozen and canned. The fresher the abalone, the more tender the flesh.

Storage: Fresh abalone will live for 3–5 days if kept in a bucket covered with a bag soaked in sea water. If the abalone is dead when purchased, shuck as soon as possible and refrigerate. Store in airtight container for 2–3 days. Store frozen for up to 3 months. Can be kept in an aerated aquarium, and thus taken fresh from the water.

Preparation: To shuck, use a strong lever and force tip in thin end of shell under the flesh. Wiggle lever until muscle comes free. Remove meat and wash well; remove intestine; trim off any dark portions. Cut with a sharp knife into thin slices (about 9mm-thick). Pound each slice with a wooden mallet (until limp and velvety). May be chopped and minced rather than sliced.

Cooking: If cooking the whole abalone, the cleaned shell may be used as the cooking utensil. Place meat back in shell, place selected flavourings on top, and steam for 2–3 hours. Discard flavourings, and serve in shell. Can be braised, pan-fried, deep-fried, poached or stewed. If pan-frying, cook quickly over high heat. Do not overcook.

Sweet-Cooked Abalone

Ingredients
500mL can abalone (packed in water)
150mL cold water
2½ tablespoons saké wine
30g sugar
2½ teaspoons MasterFoods Soy Sauce

Method
1. Empty can of abalone into small saucepan, and add the water. Bring to the boil, then lower the heat and simmer (uncovered) for 10 minutes.

2. Add the saké and sugar, and cook (for another 5 minutes), then stir in the soy sauce, and cook for 2–3 minutes longer.

3. Cool to room temperature, then cut the abalone into slices (1cm-thick), and serve as cold finger food or succulent first course.

Serves 4

Pan-Fried Abalone Steaks

Ingredients
250g abalone steaks (prepared as page 10)
65g cornflour
2 eggs
2 tablespoons lemon juice
3 tablespoons butter

Method
1. Coat abalone steaks well with cornflour. Dip into mixture of lightly beaten eggs and lemon juice.

2. Preheat shallow frypan and melt butter, then fry steaks very quickly. (About 45–60 seconds on each side is long enough; it is very important not to overcook because meat will toughen.)

Serves 2–4

Abalone Stew

Ingredients
500g abalone steaks (prepared as on page 10)
90g butter (unsalted)
125g onion (finely chopped)
1 teaspoon MasterFoods Freshly Crushed Garlic
65g red capsicum
65g green capsicum
1 MasterFoods Bay Leaf
250g jar MasterFoods Tomato Paste
500mL water
3 potatoes (peeled and cut into 5mm-cubes)
½ teaspoon salt
⅓ teaspoon MasterFoods Ground Cayenne Pepper

Method
1. Cut abalone into 1cm-cubes, and reserve. In a large saucepan (over medium heat) melt butter, and sauté onion, garlic and capsicum until onion is opaque (about 5 minutes). Add bayleaf, tomato paste, water, potatoes, salt and cayenne.

2. Cover and simmer until potatoes are almost tender (about 15 minutes). Add abalone cubes, and simmer until tender (about 4–5 minutes).

3. Serve immediately.

Serves 6–8

Abalone Chowder

Ingredients

2 slices bacon (cut into 2.5cm-pieces)
1 medium onion (chopped)
3 teaspoons MasterFoods Freshly Crushed Garlic
2 stalks celery (chopped)
1 large carrot (chopped)
½ teaspoon MasterFoods Freshly Chopped Chilli
440g can tomato pieces
2 tablespoons MasterFoods Tomato Paste
2 MasterFoods Bay Leaves
1 heaped teaspoon MasterFoods Thyme Leaves
½ teaspoon salt
½ teaspoon MasterFoods Black Peppercorns (freshly
        ground)
250mL basic fish stock (page 39)
1½ litres water
500g abalone steaks (ground or finely chopped)
2 medium pontiac potatoes (diced)
2 tablespoons plain flour
2 tablespoons water
2 ice cubes
125mL dry sherry

Method

1. Fry bacon in a large frypan (until crisp). Pour off almost all fat, keeping a small amount. Fry onion, garlic, celery, carrot and chilli in the remaining bacon fat.

2. Cook for 3–4 minutes (until vegetables are tender). Add the tomatoes, including the juice, tomato paste, bay leaves, thyme and salt and pepper. Stir in the fish stock, water, abalone and potatoes. Bring the mixture to boiling, then reduce heat to simmer. Simmer uncovered for 40–45 minutes.

3. In a jar with a tight-fitting lid, combine the flour, water and ice cubes. Shake the jar vigorously, then pour the flour and water paste into the chowder. Add the sherry. Stir and increase the heat (until the liquid boils). Allow the mixture to boil gently (until the broth thickens slightly).

4. Taste for seasoning, and add more sherry and salt and pepper (if desired).

Serves 10

CRAB

(Blue Swimmer, Mud, Mangrove, Spanner, Giant, Frog, Blue, Snow)

A number of types of crab are covered by this heading. Crabmeat is believed by many to be the most succulent of all the shellfish, the most sought-after being the mud, blue swimmer and, to a lesser extent, spanner crab.

Availability: Crabs are available all year round, with restrictions on the supply of some varieties during the breeding season. Uncooked mud crabs must be supplied live as the flesh tends to spoil quickly after death. Blue Swimmers are normally supplied cooked as they have a very short life after capture. Spanner crabs are available both live and cooked.

Storage: Uncooked mud crabs will survive several days out of water. Keep in a damp hessian bag in a cool dark place. Cooked crabs can be wrapped in foil and kept in refrigerator for up to 3 days. Freeze for up to 3 months.

Preparation: Never put live crabs in boiling water as the meat will toughen and the legs and claws could fall off. Check killing and cleaning methods in the preparation section (page 64).

Cooking: One of the best methods of cooking mud crab is by poaching in salted water (25g salt per litre), with lemon and black pepper: cook for about 8 minutes per 500g (once water is simmering). The crab can then be finished off for the final dish by a variety of methods, including barbecuing or pan-frying. In Chinese cooking, mud crab is a delight when poached with black bean or chilli.

Crabmeat Ramekins

Ingredients
500g crabmeat
3 rashers bacon
1 teaspoon MasterFoods Mustard Powder
1 teaspoon MasterFoods Ground Paprika
1 teaspoon MasterFoods Celery Salt
Tabasco sauce
2 tablespoons sweet chilli sauce
1 teaspoon white wine vinegar
1 cup mayonnaise
MasterFoods Parsley Flakes (for garnish)

Method
1. Preheat oven to moderate temperature (180°C).

2. Divide crab among 6 greased ramekins, and place in moderate oven to heat through.

3. Chop bacon, and fry (until crisp). Sprinkle over crab.

4. Combine mustard, paprika, celery salt, 2 drops Tabasco sauce, chilli sauce, vinegar and mayonnaise.

5. Spoon over crabmeat, and brown under a hot griller (until golden). Garnish with chopped parsley.

Serves 6

Blue Swimmer Special

Ingredients
olive oil
4 teaspoons MasterFoods Freshly Crushed Garlic
6 blue swimmer cabs (cut in half)
1kg tomatoes (fresh, peeled and mashed)
1 can tomato puree
1 tablespoon MasterFoods Sweet Basil Leaves
3 teaspoons sugar
2 tablespoons MasterFoods Parsley Flakes
salt and freshly ground MasterFoods Black Peppercorns

Method
1. Cover bottom of large saucepan with olive oil. Add garlic, and heat gently.

2. Add crabs, and cook over a moderate heat (for 10 minutes).

3. Add rest of ingredients, bring to boil, reduce heat and simmer (for 30 minutes).

Serves 4-6

Hot Crab Salad

Ingredients
2 tablespoons oil
120g butter
200g mushrooms (sliced)
6 shallots (chopped)
½ red capsicum (cut in small dice)
1 cup rice (cooked)
125g water chestnuts (cut in half)
2 teaspoons lemon juice
500g mud crabmeat
salt and MasterFoods Cracked Black Peppercorns
2 tablespoons MasterFoods Parsley Flakes

Method
1. Heat oil and butter in frypan, sauté mushrooms, shallots and capsicum for 3-5 minutes.

2. Add rice, mix well, and cook (stirring) over moderate heat.

3. Add water chestnuts, lemon juice and crabmeat. Season to taste with salt and pepper.

4. Sprinkle with parsley to serve.

Serves 4-6

Crabmeat Fritters

Ingredients

3 eggs
1 cup bean sprouts
400g crabmeat
salt and MasterFoods Cracked Black Peppercorns
oil (for deep frying)

Sauce:

2 teaspoons cornflour
1 tablespoon sugar
3 tablespoons MasterFoods Soy Sauce
1 MasterFoods Squeeze-On Chicken Stock
250mL water
2 tablespoons dry sherry

Method

1. Beat the eggs in a bowl, stir in bean sprouts and crabmeat, and add salt and pepper (to taste).

2. Heat sufficient oil to cover the base of a frying pan, and drop in all of the crab mixture (a heaped tablespoon at a time).

3. Fry until golden brown on one side, then turn and brown the other side.

4. Remove from pan, and keep warm.

5. **Sauce:** Blend together the cornflour and sugar in a pan, add soy sauce, crumbled stock cube and water.

6. Slowly bring to the boil over a low heat (stirring all the time). Cook for 3 minutes (or until sauce is thickened). Stir in sherry.

Serves 4

Stuffed Crab Mushrooms

Ingredients

8 mushrooms (each about 5cm-diameter; stem removed)
French dressing for marinating
200g crabmeat
2 tablespoons red capsicum (finely chopped)
2 tablespoons celery (finely chopped)
1 teaspoon lemon juice
¼ teaspoon MasterFoods Original Dijon Mustard*
pinch MasterFoods Dill Leaf Tips
2 tablespoons sour cream
3 tablespoons mayonnaise*

Method

1. Marinate mushrooms in French dressing for about 30 minutes.

2. Place crabmeat, capsicum and celery in a bowl. Lightly mix together.

3. Blend remaining ingredients together, and mix through crab mixture. Chill.

4. Just before serving, drain mushroom caps and fill with crab mixture.

Serves 4

> ### *Jan's Handy Hint
> Try substituting 4 tablespoons of Master Foods Dijonaise for Dijon mustard and mayonnaise in this recipe—the result is fabulous!

Devilled Crab Cakes

Ingredients

200g crabmeat
2 teaspoons Worcestershire Sauce
2 teaspoons MasterFoods American Mustard
dash Tabasco
1 teaspoon MasterFoods Freshly Crushed Garlic
salt and MasterFoods Cracked Black Peppercorns
2 slices bread (crusts removed)
65mL milk
1 egg (beaten)
plain flour
2 tablespoons oil
30g butter
fresh parsley (for garnish)

Method

1. Combine flaked crabmeat, Worcestershire sauce, mustard, Tabasco, garlic, salt and pepper.

2. Soak bread in milk then squeeze out milk. Add to crab with beaten egg, and mix well.

3. Shape into 4 cakes, and dust lightly with flour.

4. Heat oil and butter in a frying pan. Add the crab-cakes, and fry until golden brown (about 3 minutes each side).

5. Garnish with chopped parsley.

Serves 2 (as a main course) or 4 (as an entrée)

Sherried Crabmeat

Ingredients

250g mushrooms
3 tablespoons butter
2 tablespoons butter (extra)
3 tablespoons flour
250mL chicken stock
125mL cream
500g crabmeat (flaked)
65g Parmesan cheese
salt and MasterFoods Cracked Black Peppercorns
2 tablespoons dry sherry
vol au vent cases

Method

1. Sauté mushrooms in 2 tablespoons butter, and set aside.

2. Melt extra butter and stir in flour, cook (stirring) for 2 minutes.

3. Over low heat stir in chicken stock and cream. When sauce is boiling, add crabmeat and mushrooms.

4. When sauce comes to second boil, add Parmesan cheese and season with salt and pepper.

5. Remove from heat and add sherry. Spoon into heated vol au vent cases.

Serves 4–6

Baked Crab and Prawns

Ingredients

500g crabmeat
500g prawns (cooked)
125g shallots (chopped)
125g red capsicum (chopped)
125g celery (chopped)
4 tablespoons lemon juice
3 tablespoons MasterFoods Sweet Thai Chilli Sauce
250mL mayonnaise
buttered bread crumbs

Method

1. Preheat oven to moderate temperature (180°C).

2. Combine all ingredients (except breadcrumbs) in a greased casserole dish. Top with buttered breadcrumbs.

3. Cook in a moderate oven for 25–30 minutes (or until bubbly-hot).

Serves 4–6

Crab Casseroles

Ingredients

20g butter
1 onion (chopped)
1 green capsicum (diced)
400g crabmeat
200mL mayonnaise
4 hard boiled eggs (chopped)
250g cooked rice
1½ cups fresh breadcrumbs
1 tablespoon MasterFoods Parsley Flakes
45g butter (melted)

Method

1. Preheat oven (to 180°C).

2. Heat butter in pan, add onion and capsicum, and stir over a moderate heat (until onions are soft).

3. Stir in crab, mayonnaise, eggs and rice.

4. Spoon mixture into an ovenproof dish. Mix together breadcrumbs, parsley and melted butter.

5. Sprinkle breadcrumb mix over crab mixture. Bake in a moderate oven for 20–25 minutes.

Serves 4

Crab in Creamy Tomato Sauce

Ingredients

30g butter
1kg crabmeat
3 teaspoons MasterFoods Freshly Crushed Garlic
250g fresh parsley(chopped)
2 tablespoons lemon juice
2 tablespoons MasterFoods Tomato Paste
250mL cream
salt and pepper

Method

1. Melt butter in a frying pan. Add crabmeat, garlic and parsley, and cook over low heat for 2–3 minutes.

2. Stir in lemon juice, tomato paste and cream. Season with salt and pepper. Heat gently.

Serves 4–6

Crab with Ginger

Ingredients

2 x 750g or 1 x 1.5kg fresh mud crab
1 tablespoon corn oil
60g fresh peeled ginger (thinly sliced and cut into strips)
1 teaspoon MasterFoods Freshly Crushed Garlic
5 shallots (cut into 5cm-pieces)
250mL basic fish stock (page 39)
1 tablespoon dry sherry
1 teaspoon oyster sauce
½ teaspoon Worcestershire sauce
1 tablespoon MasterFoods Soy Sauce
½ teaspoon sugar
2 teaspoons cornflour (mixed with 1 tablespoon cold water)
1 teaspoon sesame oil
1 red chilli (slivered; for garnish)
boiled rice (for serving)

Method

1. Steam crab for 8 minutes over vigorously boiling water. Remove crab, let cool, then remove the top shell and clean. Cut the body in half and remove legs and claws. Set aside.

2. Preheat wok or large skillet, then heat oil, add ginger and stir-fry until the ginger is fragrant (about 30 seconds).

3. Add the garlic and shallots with the crab pieces, and stir-fry (for about 1 minute).

4. Combine the stock, sherry, oyster sauce, Worcestershire sauce, soy sauce and sugar, and pour into the wok. Cover and cook (over medium heat) for 3 minutes.

5. Remove the crab with tongs, and set aside on plate.

6. Add the dissolved cornflour to the wok and cook (stirring) until the sauce thickens (about 1 minute).

7. Pour the sauce and shallot mixture onto a serving platter, reassemble the crab, and place the shell over the body to give the impression of a whole crab lying on the platter.

8. Trickle sesame oil over the surface, garnish with chilli slivers, and serve with boiled rice on the side.

Serves 4

Mud Crab

Chilli Crab

Ingredients

2 x 750g mud crabs (cooked; see Step 1 of Crab with
    Ginger method, page 66)
3 teaspoons MasterFoods Freshly Chopped Chilli
1 small red chilli (chopped)
2 teaspoons MasterFoods Freshly Chopped Ginger
3 teaspoons MasterFoods Freshly Crushed Garlic
125mL vegetable oil
310mL chunky-style tomato sauce
2 tablespoons brown sugar
160mL boiling water
salt
1 egg (beaten)
fresh coriander leaves (for garnish)

Accompaniments:

1 cucumber (cut into chunks)
crisp French bread (cut into thick slices)

Method

1. Remove the large claws from each crab and crack
   at the joints. Use a hammer (or rolling pin) and crack
   the broadest part of the shell cleanly (taking care not
   to splinter shell). Turn each crab on its back with its
   tail-flap towards you. Tap around the fault line with a
   hammer and push the body out of each shell. Discard
   the stomach sac and the lungs.

2. Leave the creamy brown meat in the shell, and break
   in half. Cut the lower half of the body in half and
   crack the smaller claws.

3. Pound the fresh chillies, ginger and garlic to a fine
   paste with a mortar and pestle (or chop up in a food
   processor).

4. Heat the oil in a hot wok (or a heavy-bottomed
   saucepan), add the paste, and cook gently without
   browning (or until the mixture gives off a spicy
   aroma).

5. Add tomato sauce, brown sugar, 160mL boiling water
   and salt (to taste).

6. When sauce is bubbling, toss in the crabs, and mix to
   ensure the crabs are coated in the sauce. Add the
   beaten egg (which will become almost scrambled in
   the sauce).

7. Spoon onto a warmed serving bowl, and sprinkle with
   coriander leaves.

8. Serve immediately, with the cucumber and bread
   accompaniments.

Serves 4

LOBSTER

Rock Lobster is the marketing name (Southern Rock, Crayfish, Spiny, Cray, Eastern Tropical Rock, Painted Rock, Western Rock, Coral Cray)

The rock lobster is highly sought-after for both local consumption and export sales. They vary in size from 340g to1360g. Caught all around the coastline of Australia.

Availability: Lobsters are available all-year-round. Available uncooked (green), whole and alive, or frozen as lobster tails and lobster meat. Cooked: whole, or as frozen portions.

Storage: Keep live lobster in a damp hessian bag in a cool, dark place. Cooked lobster can be wrapped in foil and kept in refrigerator for up to 3 days. Freeze up to 3 months.

Preparation: See preparation, killing and cleaning methods (on page 64).

Cooking: Never put live lobster in boiling water as the meat will toughen (and the legs and claws could fall off). Place lobster in cold water (after killing, as instructed on page 64), and bring slowly to the boil. Allow 8 minutes per 500g (but do not overcook). To grill green lobster tails, just make a couple of slits on the underside of the tail with a sharp knife, to allow heat penetration. Place on barbecue (or under grill) and brush with butter. Grill 20cm from heat for about 5–8 minutes each side.

Lobster Bisque

Ingredients
2 cooked lobster tails
1.5 litres chicken stock
30g butter
1 tablespoon onion (chopped)
2 tablespoons plain flour
2 tablespoons brandy
2 tablespoons sherry
1 tablespoon MasterFoods Tomato Paste
2 teaspoons MasterFoods Ground Cayenne Pepper
85mL cream

Method
1. Remove meat from lobster tails and flake with a fork. Bring stock and lobster shells to the boil, reduce heat, cover, simmer 30 minutes. Strain, and reserve stock.

2. Melt butter in a saucepan, add onion, stir over heat until brown. Add flour, cook (stirring) for 1 minute.

3. Stir in stock, brandy, sherry, tomato paste and cayenne pepper. Bring to the boil and add lobster meat. Reduce heat, and simmer (for 10 minutes). Add cream and heat through.

Serves 6

Jan's Handy Tip
Lobster is the monarch of seafood. It has a light, sweet, rich taste which is popular with even the most discerning palate. Renowned for its succulent flesh and spectacular appearance, the rock lobster is a must for the seafood connoisseur.

Lobster Thermidor

Ingredients
4 raw lobster tails
15g butter
1½ tablespoons plain flour
250mL milk
2 teaspoons MasterFoods German Mustard
1 teaspoon MasterFoods Wholegrain Mustard
65mL cream

Crunchy Topping:
2 tablespoons Parmesan cheese (grated)
65g breadcrumbs (stale)
1 tablespoon MasterFoods Chopped Chives
½ teaspoon lemon rind (grated)
15g butter (melted)

Method
1. Remove flesh from tails, and chop flesh into bite-sized pieces. Add lobster shells to large saucepan of boiling water, and cook for 1 minute (or until shells change colour). Drain shells, rinse under cold water, and dry.

2. Melt butter in saucepan, stir in flour, stir over moderate heat (for 1 minute). Remove from heat and gradually add milk (stirring constantly). Cook until mixture boils and thickens.

3. Stir in mustards and lobster flesh, cook over medium heat for about 2 minutes (or until lobster is cooked).

4. Remove from heat, and stir in cream. Spoon mixture into lobster shells, and sprinkle with topping. Grill until lightly browned.

5. **Crunchy Topping:** Combine all ingredients in small bowl.

Serves 4

Jan's Handy Tip
Boiled, baked or barbecued, grilled, steamed or sliced for sashimi, rock lobsters make an excellent seafood dish. Their exotic appearance sets them apart, so take care not to damage the legs and head during preparation.

Popular sauces to accompany rock lobster are thermidor, mornay and Newburg, but suggestions for other complementary tastes abound. Try sweet corn, citrus fruits, chillies, tarragon butter sauces, garlic and white wine, coconut milk or curries. Perhaps combine in quenelles and mousselines. Prepare as a bisque or serve in a salad with other seafood, or on its own with fresh green peppercorns and chargrilled pineapple.

To enhance the flavour when cooking rock lobster in liquid, try a classic Court Bouillon (page 84) instead of water.

Lobster Mornay

Ingredients

1 medium lobster (cooked; halved)

Mornay Sauce:

310mL milk
1 bay leaf
1 small onion (chopped)
5 black MasterFoods Black Peppercorns
30g butter
2 tablespoons plain flour
65mL cream
65g cheese (grated)
salt and MasterFoods Cracked Black Peppercorns
15g butter (extra; melted)
65g breadcrumbs (fresh)

Serves 2

Method

1. Remove lobster meat from shells and cut into bite-sized pieces. Reserve shells.
2. In a saucepan, place milk, bay leaf, onion and peppercorns. Heat slowly to boiling point. Remove from heat, cover and stand for 10 minutes. Strain.
3. In a pan: heat butter, and remove from heat. Stir in flour and blend, gradually adding strained milk. Return pan to heat, and stir constantly (until sauce boils and thickens). Simmer sauce for 1 minute. Remove from heat, add cream, cheese, salt and pepper. Stir sauce (until cheese melts), and add lobster.
4. Divide mixture between shells. Melt extra butter in a small pan, add breadcrumbs, and stir to combine.
5. Scatter crumbs over lobster and brown under a hot grill.

Lobster Newburg

Ingredients

60g butter
2kg lobster (boiled, shelled and cut into small pieces)
2 teaspoons salt
¼ teaspoon MasterFoods Ground Cayenne Pepper
¼ teaspoon MasterFoods Ground Nutmeg
250mL double cream
4 egg yolks
2 tablespoons brandy
2 tablespoons dry sherry
reserved lobster-tail shell or 4–6 vol-au-vent cases and
    rice (for serving)

Serves 4–6

Method

1. In a shallow frypan melt butter over a moderate heat. When the foam subsides, add lobster.

2. Cook slowly (for about 5 minutes). Add the salt, cayenne pepper and nutmeg.

3. In a small bowl lightly beat the cream with the egg yolks. Add the mixture to the pan (stirring continuously).

4. Finally, add the brandy and sherry (as the mass begins to thicken). Do not allow to boil (because the sauce will curdle).

5. Serve either (i) placed back in the lobster tail shell; or (ii) in vol-au-vent cases. Serve with steamed rice in shell (or vol-au-vent cases).

Lobster Provençale

Ingredients

60g butter
1 teaspoon MasterFoods Freshly Crushed Garlic
2 spring onions (chopped)
300g can tomatoes
salt and MasterFoods Cracked Black Peppercorns (to taste)
pinch of MasterFoods Saffron
1 large cooked lobster
60mL brandy
boiled rice
½ bunch fresh chives (chopped, for garnish)
lemon wedges (for garnish)

Serves 4

Method

1. In a shallow frypan: melt butter over a moderate heat. Add garlic, spring onions, tomatoes, salt and pepper, and saffron. Cook until onions are translucent (about 2 minutes).

2. Remove meat from lobster, and cut into large pieces. Add lobster to frypan, and flame with the brandy. Cook gently (until lobster is heated through).

3. Place rice on serving plate, and sprinkle with chives.

4. Remove lobster from frypan (retaining the cooking liquid as a sauce).

5. Arrange the lobster on the rice and spoon sauce (which has been cooked with the lobster) over lobster. Serve with lemon wedges on side of plate.

OCTOPUS

**Octopus is the marketing name
(Southern, Pale, Maori, Gloomy, Brown,
White, Pink)**

*Octopus is an increasingly popular seafood,
especially for barbecues.*

*Has 8 tentacles and no internal backbone. Caught
all around Australia.*

Availability: Available in various sizes; whole, all-year-round; fresh or frozen.

Storage: Clean before storing and refrigerate wrapped in GLAD Wrap or airtight GLAD Snap Lock Bags. Will keep up to 2 days in refrigerator and will store in freezer for up to 3 months.

Preparation: See preparation methods for octopus (on page 11).

Cooking: Simmer until fork-tender about (1–2 hours), in half red wine and half olive oil. Great for grill or barbecue. Marinate in one of the recommended marinades on page 84.

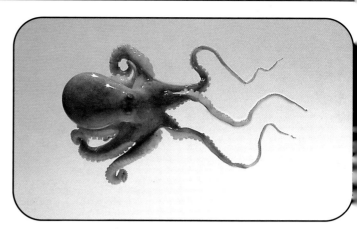

Barbecued Octopus with Capsicum Salad

Ingredients

500g baby octopus
65mL olive oil
125mL lemon juice
1 teaspoon MasterFoods Ground Oregano Leaves or
   Marjoram Leaves
1 teaspoon MasterFoods Freshly Crushed Garlic
1 medium-sized green capsicum
1 medium-sized red capsicum
1 medium-sized yellow capsicum
extra oil (for brushing capsicums)

Method

1. Cut octopus hood into strips. Cut tentacles into 2.5cm-pieces. (If octopus is very small they may be left whole.) Wash well, pat dry and place in a glass bowl.

2. Add oil, lemon juice, herbs and garlic. Cover, place in the refrigerator, and allow to marinate for 24 hours. Turn in the marinade occasionally.

3. Cut capsicums into four (lengthways), and remove the seeds and the white membrane. Brush outer skin with extra oil and place (skin-side-down) on a hot barbecue (until skins are well blistered). Rub off skins with a towel. Arrange on a platter or individual plates, alternating the colours. Drizzle with half of the marinade, and set aside.

4. Reduce barbecue to medium heat. Place octopus on the barbecue plate and cook for 15–20 minutes (turning frequently, and splashing on a little marinade as they cook).

5. Remove, and pile into the centre of the capsicum salad. Pour remaining dressing over the dish, and serve.

Serves 4–6

Jan's Handy Tip

The octopus is not the frightening fish so popular with Hollywood movies. It is more of a shy, retiring mollusc (and, like the squid, is a cephalopod). It has a very sweet and flavoursome meat that is generally undervalued. Delicious grilled or stewed, but must be tenderised prior to cooking. Best ways are to simmer it for 45 minutes, or slice thinly and pound with a wooden mallet. (See previous pages for cleaning details.)

Octopus Stew

Ingredients

6 tablespoons olive oil
1kg octopus (cleaned and cut into small pieces;
   cleaning technique page 11)
salt and MasterFoods Cracked Black Peppercorns (to
   taste)
1 leek (chopped)
1 onion (chopped)
1 stick celery (chopped)
¼ teaspoon MasterFoods Thyme Leaves
¼ teaspoon fennel
1 MasterFoods Bay Leaf
4 medium tomatoes (skinned, seeded and chopped)
¼ teaspoon MasterFoods Saffron
1 teaspoon MasterFoods Freshly Crushed Garlic
175g long-grain rice

Method

1. Heat oil in an ovenproof casserole dish. Toss in the octopus pieces, and sauté over a brisk heat (seasoning to taste with pepper). When the pieces are golden, add the leek, onion, celery and herbs. As soon as the leek starts to turn golden, add the tomatoes, saffron and garlic.

2. Add enough water to cover the contents of the casserole by about 1cm. Cover, and cook over low heat for 1 hour (adding water from time-to-time to keep water level constant). About 20 minutes before serving, add the rice.

3. Serve from casserole (or from heated serving dish).

Serves 4

Spicy Marinade

Ingredients

60mL tomato sauce
2 teaspoons malt vinegar
2 teaspoons MasterFoods Soy Sauce
2 teaspoons honey
2 teaspoons olive oil
2 teaspoons MasterFoods Freshly Crushed Garlic
2 teaspoons MasterFoods Freshly Chopped Ginger
2 teaspoons MasterFoods Sweet Thai Chilli Sauce

Method

1. Place all ingredients in a bowl and mix well to combine.

This is an ideal marinade for barbecued octopus. Just clean octopus as page 11 and marinate in liquid for minimum 8 hours in refrigerator.

Should be enough for 1.5kg octopus.

Octopus with Potatoes and Peas

Ingredients

1kg octopus (cleaned, skinned; cleaning technique
    page 11)
salt
150mL olive oil
1 large onion (chopped)
4 garlic cloves (chopped)
400g can tomatoes
¼ teaspoon MasterFoods Ground Chillies
500g potatoes (peeled and cut into thick slices)
250g cooked peas

Method

1. Put octopus in a large saucepan without adding
   water. Sprinkle with salt, cover, and let cook in its own
   juices over a low heat (for about 45 minutes).

2. Four times during the cooking, lift the octopus out
   (using a fork) and dip into a pan of boiling water;
   then run the octopus under cold water and return it
   to the saucepan to continue cooking.

3. Heat olive oil in an ovenproof casserole dish and
   gently fry in it the onion, garlic, tomatoes and chilli
   powder for about 10 minutes (or until the onion has
   turned opaque). Add the potatoes and cook for
   about 5 minutes. Add the octopus and enough of its
   cooking liquid to cover the contents of the casserole.
   Add salt as desired, and let the dish cook gently,
   uncovered for about 30 minutes (or until the potatoes
   are tender and the sauce is largely reduced).

4. Finally, add the cooked peas to the casserole and
   heat through. Serve the octopus and vegetables
   straight from the casserole.

Serves 4

OYSTER
(Sydney Rock, Native, Pacific, Flat, Angasi)

Most oysters supplied are of the farmed variety. Some natural oysters are still available. However, one has to be extremely lucky to come across a natural oyster-bed.

Availability: Sold raw in the shell or half-shell. May be shucked, bottled or smoked.

Storage: Fresh unshucked oysters may be left in a bucket in a cool, wet place covered with hessian, where they will remain fresh for up to two weeks. In half-shell, place on crushed ice in refrigerator and cover with GLAD Wrap.

Preparation: See preparation methods for oysters (on page 65).

Cooking: The best 'cooking' style with oysters is 'au natural', served with lemon, pepper and salt (and a little seafood sauce on the side). For numerous ways to cook and enjoy oysters, follow some of the recipes on these pages.

Oyster Kebabs
Ingredients
1 large bottle fresh oysters
plain flour, salt and pepper
12 bamboo skewers (soaked in water for 30 minutes)
2 eggs (lightly beaten)
2 cups breadcrumbs (fresh)
2 tablespoons MasterFoods Parsley Flakes
oil (for deep frying)

Seafood Sauce:
4 tablespoons thickened cream
1 tablespoon tomato sauce
1 tablespoon lemon juice
2 tablespoons Worcestershire sauce
dash Tabasco
½ teaspoon MasterFoods Horseradish Cream
pinch dry mustard
salt and MasterFoods Cracked Black Peppercorns

Method
1. Drain oysters, toss in seasoned flour. Gently push oysters onto bamboo skewers.

2. Coat kebabs in beaten egg, then roll in breadcrumbs combined with chopped parsley.

3. Heat oil in frying pan. Fry quickly for about 1 minute (or until crumbs are golden).

4. Serve with seafood sauce.

5. **Seafood Sauce:** Combine all ingredients thoroughly.

Serves 4–6

Jan's Handy Tip
Oyster sauce has become a popular cooking sauce, especially when used with Chinese vegetables (most particularly *bok choy*). It is made from a concentrate of cooked oysters, soy sauce and brine, and is a thick brown sauce with a rich flavour. Can also be used as a condiment.

Baked Oysters with Bacon
Ingredients
1 clove garlic (crushed)
40g butter
120g fresh breadcrumbs
salt and pepper to taste
24 oysters (bottled or fresh)
3 bacon rashers

Method
1. Preheat oven to hot temperature (210–220°C).

2. Sauté garlic in butter 1-2 minutes. Add breadcrumbs, salt and pepper, and fry (until just turning brown).

3. Drain oysters, and place in a shallow, greased ovenproof dish.

4. Cover all over with browned crumbs, and place strips of bacon over top.

5. Put in hot oven (until bacon is browned and crisp).

Serves 4

Baked Oysters
Ingredients
40g butter
200g fresh breadcrumbs
1 teaspoon MasterFoods Freshly Crushed Garlic
1 tablespoon MasterFoods Parsley Flakes
2 dozen fresh oysters
65g Parmesan cheese (freshly grated)
30g butter (extra)

Method
1. Preheat oven to hot (210–220°C).

2. Grease an ovenproof platter (just large enough to hold the oysters in a single layer).

3. Melt butter in a frypan over a moderate heat. When the foam subsides, add the breadcrumbs and garlic and toss (until golden). Stir in the parsley.

4. Spread about two-thirds of the breadcrumb mixture in the bottom of the platter and arrange the oysters over it.

5. Mix the rest of the breadcrumbs with the grated cheese and spread over the oysters.

6. Dot the top with the extra butter chopped into tiny pieces.

7. Bake in the preheated hot oven for 15 minutes (or until top is golden).

Serves 6–8

Creamed Oysters

Ingredients

1 large bottle oysters
2 tablespoons butter
2 tablespoons plain flour
125mL milk
65mL cream
pinch MasterFoods Ground Cayenne Pepper
2 tablespoons dry sherry
salt to taste
4 slices toast (hot, buttered)
MasterFoods Parsley Flakes (to garnish)

Method

1. Drain oysters (reserving ¼ cup liquid).

2. Melt butter in saucepan, stir in flour, and cook (for 2 minutes) over low heat.

3. Slowly stir-in milk, cream and reserved oyster liquid. Add cayenne pepper, sherry and salt (to taste). Simmer for 2 minutes.

4. Add oysters, and simmer another minute or two (until oysters are just plump).

5. Spoon over toast and sprinkle with parsley.

Serves 4

Oysters Greta Garbo

(photographed below)

Ingredients

3 dozen natural oysters in shells
juice of ½ lime or lemon
6 slices smoked salmon (cut into fine strips)
250mL sour cream
2 tablespoons chives (fresh, chopped; for garnish)
red caviar (for garnish)
crushed ice (for serving)

Method

1. Sprinkle the oysters with lime juice and top with smoked salmon.

2. Dollop the sour cream onto each oyster.

3. Garnish with chives and red caviar. Serve on a bed of ice.

Serves 6 (as an entrée)

Jan's Handy Tip
When buying oysters, ensure that they are plump and shiny with a natural creamy colour and clear liquid. Fresh unopened oysters may be kept in a cool place in a wet bag for up to 14 days.

Oysters Greta Garbo

PRAWN

(King, Red Spot, Greentail, Western King, Royal Red, Brown Tiger, School, Easter King, Banana, White, Grooved Tiger, Black Tiger, Endeavour, Bay)

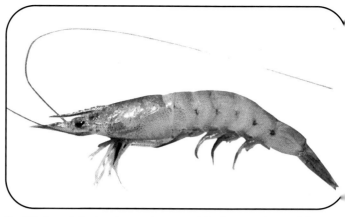

Prawns are the most popular seafood in Australia. Caught all around the coastline, this vast range of species is always in demand for both local and export consumption.

Availability: Available all-year-round, green (raw) or cooked, shelled, unshelled, fresh or frozen. Vary in size from Bay Prawn (5cm in length) to King Prawn (over 11cm in length).

Storage: In shell in refrigerator in a plastic bag or airtight container. Will keep for up to 3 days in refrigerator and will store in freezer for up to 3 months.

Preparation: See preparation methods (on page 65).

Cooking: Very versatile, prawns may be boiled, grilled, stir-fried, deep-fried, baked or barbecued. Used in salads and cocktails after cooking and chilling. Green prawns may be cooked in any of the above ways. To boil green prawns, place in boiling salted water (25g salt per litre). Boil until a nice pinkish/red shade about 3–5 minutes. Do not overcook as the flesh will toughen.

Prawns in Tomato Sauce
Ingredients
50g butter
1 large onion (finely chopped)
1 teaspoon MasterFoods Freshly Crushed Garlic
4 large ripe tomatoes (skinned and chopped)
1 tablespoon MasterFoods Tomato Paste
500mL dry white wine
1 MasterFoods Bay Leaf
salt and pepper
1kg prawns
6 shallots (chopped)

Method
1. Heat butter in pan, and add onion and garlic. Cook until onion is soft.

2. Add tomatoes, tomato paste, wine and bayleaf, and season (to taste) with salt and pepper. Bring to boil, reduce heat, and simmer (uncovered) for 30 minutes (or until sauce is reduced and thickened). Remove bay leaf.

3. Add shelled prawns and chopped shallots, and simmer gently (until prawns are heated through).

Serves 4

Almond Crumbed Prawns
Ingredients
750g green king prawns
65g plain flour
1 egg
85mL milk
250g almonds (blanched)
oil (for deep frying)

Method
1. Shell prawns (leaving tails intact, but remove vein). Cut prawns down back, and spread out flat.

2. Sift flour into basin, make a well in the centre, add combined beaten egg and milk, and gradually stir in flour. Beat until smooth.

3. Dip prawns into batter, and then roll in finely chopped almonds.

4. Drop into hot oil, and fry (until golden brown).

Serves 4–6

Garlic Lemon Prawns
Ingredients
500g green king prawns
1 teaspoon lemon rind (grated)
2 tablespoons lemon juice
1 teaspoon MasterFoods Freshly Crushed Garlic
2 teaspoons MasterFoods Lemon Pepper Seasoning
2 tablespoons olive oil
2 teaspoons MasterFoods Parsley Flakes

Method
1. Shell and devein prawns (leaving tails intact).

2. Combine lemon rind, lemon juice, garlic and lemon pepper in a bowl. Add prawns, and stir until coated.

3. Cover and refrigerate for several hours (or overnight).

4. Heat oil in a large frying pan, add prawns, and stir (until cooked through). Stir in parsley.

Serves 4

Potted Prawns
Ingredients
500g cooked prawns (peeled weight)
185g butter
¼ teaspoon MasterFoods Ground Cinnamon
¼ teaspoon MasterFoods Ground Nutmeg
1 teaspoon MasterFoods Mixed Spices (Traditional Blend)
pinch MasterFoods Ground Cayenne Pepper
freshly ground MasterFoods Black Peppercorns

Method
1. Cut prawns into small pieces.

2. Melt butter in a large frying pan and, when foam subsides, add prawns and the rest of the ingredients. Toss in butter for a few minutes.

3. Spoon into a pot (or into several small pots). Press lightly, then cover with a round piece of aluminium foil, and chill.

Serves 4

Prawn Cakes

Ingredients

30g butter
1 small onion (finely chopped)
2 tablespoons plain flour
1 teaspoon MasterFoods French Mustard
250mL light cream
salt and pepper (to taste)
500g cooked prawns (shelled and roughly chopped)
1 egg (beaten)
200g crumbs (made from savoury biscuits)
oil (for shallow frying)

Method

1. Melt butter in pan, and sauté onion over low heat (until soft).

2. Stir in flour, then mustard, cream, pepper and salt. Cook, stirring, over low heat (until sauce boils and thickens).

3. Mix in the cooked prawns. Pour into a bowl, cover and refrigerate for 2–3 hours. When mixture is well chilled, form into patties.

4. Dip patties into beaten egg, then coat with crumbs.

5. Heat oil in a large frying pan, and fry patties (until golden brown and crispy on both sides).

Serves 4

Skewered Prawns

Ingredients

500g green prawns

Marinade:

1 small onion (finely chopped)
2 teaspoons MasterFoods Freshly Crushed Garlic
1 teaspoon MasterFoods Freshly Chopped Ginger
65mL dry sherry
65mL olive oil
salt and freshly ground MasterFoods Black Peppercorns
12 bamboo skewers (soaked in water for 30 minutes)

Method

1. Wash prawns thoroughly. (Do not remove shells.)

2. Mix together ingredients to make marinade. Pour over prawns, and let stand for 1–2 hours in refrigerator.

3. Thread prawns on to skewers. Grill or barbecue for about 10 minutes (turning several times).

Serves 4

Prawns with Pineapple

Ingredients

50g butter
4 sticks celery (chopped)
1 onion (chopped)
1 red capsicum (chopped)
375mL water
1 vegetable stock cube
2 tablespoons cornflour
25mL water (extra)
1 tablespoon MasterFoods Soy Sauce
2 teaspoons lemon juice
425g can pineapple pieces (drained)
500g cooked prawns

Method

1. Heat butter in a pan, and sauté vegetables for 5 minutes.

2. Add water and crumbled stock cube. Blend cornflour with extra water, and add to pan with soy sauce and lemon juice. Stir until sauce boils and thickens.

3. Add pineapple pieces and shelled prawns. Simmer for 5 minutes.

Serves 4–6

Prawn Pâté

Ingredients

250g prawns (cooked)
45g butter
60g cream cheese
1 teaspoon MasterFoods Freshly Crushed Garlic
2 teaspoons lemon juice
1 tablespoon mayonnaise
3 drops Tabasco
¼ teaspoon MasterFoods Ground Nutmeg

Method

1. Shell and devein prawns.

2. Mash the butter and cream cheese well (until soft). Chop prawns very finely. Add the seasonings. Pack into a mould or dish.

Note: The flavour will be improved if the pâté is made a day before serving.

Serves 2–3

Prawn Salad

Ingredients

lettuce leaves
1kg cooked prawns (peeled and deveined)
1 red onion (thinly sliced)
3 avocados (peeled and sliced)

Dressing:

125mL olive oil
85mL tarragon vinegar
1 tablespoon MasterFoods Wholegrain Mustard
1 tablespoon MasterFoods Horseradish Cream
½ teaspoon MasterFoods Tarragon Leaves (crushed)
2 tablespoons tomato sauce
2 teaspoons sugar
dash MasterFoods Ground Cayenne Pepper
1 teaspoon MasterFoods Ground Paprika
65g celery (chopped)
65g shallots (chopped)

Method

1. Arrange lettuce leaves on platter, and top with prawns, onion and avocado.

2. Combine all ingredients for dressing in a container with a lid.

3. Shake well and pour (or spoon) over salad.

Serves 6–8

Prawns in Peppercorn Sauce

Ingredients

3 tablespoons butter
5 tablespoons flour
500mL milk
250mL chicken stock
pinch MasterFoods Ground Cayenne Pepper
½ teaspoon dry mustard
2 tablespoons sherry
125mL cream
1 tablespoon canned green peppercorns (rinsed)
2kg cooked medium king prawns (peeled and deveined)

Method

1. Heat butter in a large saucepan, stir in flour, and cook (stirring) for 2 minutes.
2. Over low heat, gradually stir in milk and stock, cook (stirring continuously) until mixture thickens and boils.
3. Add cayenne, mustard, sherry, cream, peppercorns and prawns. Simmer gently (until prawns are heated through).

Serves 6

Honey Ginger Prawns

Ingredients

2 tablespoons oil
1 onion (thinly sliced)
2cm-piece green ginger (grated)
1 teaspoon MasterFoods Freshly Crushed Garlic
1 green capsicum (sliced into thin strips)
500g green prawns (peeled and deveined)
125g canned water chestnuts
125mL MasterFoods Squeeze-On Chicken Stock
1 tablespoon MasterFoods Soy Sauce
1 tablespoon honey
1 teaspoon cornflour
1 tablespoon water

Method

1. Heat oil in wok. Sauté onion, ginger and garlic. Add capsicum and stir-fry for another minute (and then push to one side of wok).
2. Add prawns, and stir-fry until prawns change colour (about 2 minutes).
3. Add water chestnuts, stock, soy sauce and honey. When liquid boils, stir in the combined cornflour and water.
4. Stir until thickened and smooth.

Serves 4

Prawn Tempura

Ingredients

Batter:
2 eggs
250mL iced water
125g plain flour

oil (for deep frying)
500g uncooked prawns (shelled, tails kept intact)
chilli and soy sauces (for serving)

Method

1. Make batter by beating eggs, water and flour in a bowl (until fluffy). Set aside over ice or in freezer.
2. Heat oil. Test by dripping a small piece of bread in oil. (When it browns in 50 seconds, the oil is at its correct temperature.)
3. Dip prawns in batter and deep-fry (a few at a time) for 2–4 minutes (or until golden).
4. Serve immediately with chilli and soy sauce.

Serves 2

Peppered Prawns

Ingredients

750g green king prawns
1 small chicken stock cube
2 teaspoons cornflour
125mL water
2 tablespoons MasterFoods Soy Sauce
1 tablespoon dry sherry
2 tablespoons tomato sauce
1 teaspoon MasterFoods Freshly Crushed Garlic
2 teaspoons MasterFoods Cracked Black Peppercorns
1 tablespoon honey
2 tablespoons oil
500g broccoli (cut into flowerets)
425g can baby corn (drained)
1 onion (sliced)
1 stick celery (thinly sliced)
1 red capsicum (thinly sliced)
cornflour (extra)
1 tablespoon water (extra)

Method

1. Peel and devein prawns (leaving tails intact). Mix together the chicken stock cube, cornflour and water, and set aside.

2. Combine soy sauce, sherry, tomato sauce, garlic, pepper and honey in a large dish. Add prawns, cover, and refrigerate for several hours.

3. Heat oil in wok or large frying pan. Add vegetables, and stir-fry (for about 2 minutes).

4. Add prawns and marinade to pan, and cook (stirring) over high heat (until prawns change colour and are cooked).

5. Stir in extra cornflour (combined with extra water), and cook (stirring) until smooth.

Serves 4–6

Herbed Prawns

Ingredients

16 large green prawns
60g butter
1 tablespoon MasterFoods Parsley Flakes
1 tablespoon MasterFoods Chopped Chives (Freeze Dried)
1 teaspoon MasterFoods Dill Leaf Tips
1 tablespoon MasterFoods Sweet Thai Chilli Sauce
2 tablespoons lemon juice
1 teaspoon lemon rind (grated)
salt and freshly ground MasterFoods Black Peppercorns

Method

1. Shell and devein prawns, leaving tails intact. Melt butter in a frying pan. Add prawns. Cook over moderate heat until prawns change colour (about 3–4 minutes each side).

2. Remove pan from heat and add parsley, chives, dill, chilli sauce, lemon juice and lemon rind.

3. Season (to taste) with salt and pepper. Return to heat, and stir (to combine).

Serves 4–6

Sesame Barbecued Prawns

(photographed below)

Ingredients

1kg medium-large king prawns
65mL olive oil
65mL red wine
4 shallots (finely chopped)
1 teaspoon (grated lemon rind)
½ teaspoon MasterFoods Cracked Black Peppercorns
12 bamboo skewers (soaked in water for 30 minutes)
125g toasted MasterFoods Sesame Seeds

Method

1. Peel and devein prawns (leaving the shell tails intact).

2. Combine oil, wine, shallots, lemon rind and pepper, Mix well.

3. Thread the prawns onto bamboo skewers (approximately 3 per skewer).

4. Place the skewers in a shallow dish and pour marinade over. Allow to marinate for at least 1 hour.

5. Roll the prawns in the toasted sesame seeds, pressing them on well. Refrigerate for 30 minutes before cooking.

6. Brush with marinade during cooking.

Serves 6–8

Prawns Creole

Ingredients

1 tablespoon oil
1 small onion (roughly chopped)
4 teaspoons MasterFoods Freshly Crushed Garlic
375g tomatoes (peeled and chopped)
1 green capsicum (chopped)
6 large green olives (pitted and sliced)
1 tablespoon MasterFoods Parsley Flakes
2 teaspoons sugar
½ MasterFoods Bay Leaf
¼ teaspoon MasterFoods Thyme Leaves
½ teaspoon MasterFoods Ground Cayenne Pepper
salt (to taste)
500g medium prawns (shelled and deveined)

Method

1. Heat oil in a heavy saucepan, and sauté onion and garlic (over a medium heat) until onions are golden.

2. Add tomatoes, capsicum and olives, and sauté (for 2 minutes).

3. Add parsley, sugar, bay leaf, thyme, cayenne pepper and salt. Simmer mixture over low heat (covered) for about 20 minutes.

4. Add prawns, and cook (until they turn bright pink).

Serves 4

Sesame Barbecued Prawns

SCALLOP

(Southern, Saucer, Tasmanian, Bay, King, Queen, Sea, Commercial)

The commercial scallop (known as the Tasmanian scallop) has white meat usually surrounded by orange roe or 'coral'. The Saucer-scallop is a little less rich and is sold without the roe or 'coral'.

Availability: Sold mainly in meat form: fresh, frozen or pickled.

Storage: Store in refrigerator in an airtight container. Will keep for up to 3 days, or will freeze for up to 3 months.

Preparation: See preparation methods for scallops (on page 65).

Cooking: Pour boiling water over scallops and let stand for 2–3 minutes. Do not overcook. Very popular for barbecuing or grilling in shell, under a salamander. Encourages a myriad of cooking ideas. Try a few of the recipe suggestions on these pages.

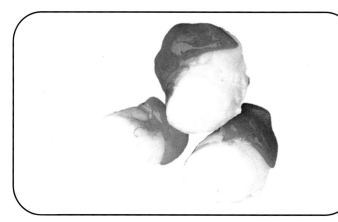

Scallops with Vegetables

Ingredients

1 teaspoon cornflour
1 tablespoon water
1 teaspoon MasterFoods Soy Sauce
½ teaspoon sugar
100g green beans
1 tablespoon oil
250g scallops
1 white onion (thinly sliced)
125g mushrooms (sliced)
125g celery (sliced)
65g bamboo shoots (thinly sliced)
125g canned pineapple pieces (drained)
250mL chicken stock

Method

1. Mix together cornflour, water, soy sauce and sugar.
2. Drop beans into boiling water, and cook for 3–4 minutes.
3. Heat about 1 tablespoon oil, and add scallops. Fry for 1 minute (stirring constantly). Remove scallops from pan.
4. Add onion, mushrooms, celery and bamboo shoots. Fry (stirring) for another 3 minutes. Add pineapple pieces, stock and beans. Cook over medium heat for 2 minutes.
5. Add scallops. Stir the cornflour mixture, add to pan, and cook (stirring) for 2 minutes.

Serves 4

Sauté of Scallops

Ingredients

30g butter
1 large onion (chopped)
2 teaspoons MasterFoods Freshly Crushed Garlic
750g scallops
3 tablespoons plain flour
1 teaspoon MasterFoods Madras Curry Powder
pepper and salt
250mL milk
MasterFoods Parsley Flakes

Method

1. In a large pan, melt the butter. Sauté onion and garlic (until onion is soft).
2. Beard scallops, and rinse well. Dry, and toss in flour mixed with curry powder, pepper and salt.
3. Sauté in pan with garlic and onion (until scallops are golden). Stir in milk.
4. Bring mixture to boil, then simmer a few minutes (or until scallops are just tender).
5. Sprinkle with chopped parsley to serve.

Serves 5–6

Creamed Scallops

Ingredients

750g scallops
250mL dry white wine
125mL water
1 teaspoon lemon juice
15g butter
1 tablespoon plain flour
250mL milk
125mL cream
salt and pepper
pinch MasterFoods Ground Cayenne Pepper
6 deep scallop shells
1 cup cheese (grated)

Method

1. Poach scallops in wine, water and lemon juice for 3–4 minutes. Cool, strain off liquid, and reserve.
2. Melt butter, add flour and cook (stirring) for 2 minutes. Gradually stir in the reserved liquid and milk. Stir until boiling.
3. Cook rapidly for 4–5 minutes. Add cream and boil again (until thick). Season with salt, pepper and cayenne pepper.
4. Add scallops and spoon into 6 deep scallop shells. Sprinkle with cheese.
5. Brown under griller.

Serves 4–6

Scallops with Plum Glaze

Ingredients

750g scallops
8 bamboo skewers
3 tablespoons plum sauce
1½ tablespoons lemon juice
½ teaspoon lemon rind (grated)
sprinkling MasterFoods Lemon Pepper Seasoning

Method

1. Wash and clean scallops. Thread evenly on 8 skewers.
2. Combine plum sauce, lemon juice, lemon rind and lemon pepper. Stir well.
3. Place scallops under grill and baste with sauce mixture. Turn once.
4. Cook for a bare minute each side.

Serves 4–6

Steamed Scallops with BlackBeans and Garlic

Ingredients

12 large scallops (or 24 small scallops)
1 tablespoon dry sherry
1 tablespoon Chinese salted black beans
1 teaspoon MasterFoods Freshly Crushed Garlic
3 teaspoons MasterFoods Soy Sauce
¼ teaspoon salt
pinch MasterFoods Cracked Black Peppercorns
½ teaspoon sugar
1 teaspoon oil
1 teaspoon cornflour
¼ teaspoon Oriental sesame oil
1 spring onion (green part only, cut into fine slices)
12 MasterFoods Coriander Leaves
½ hot chilli (seeded; cut into 5mm-diamond shapes)

Serves 4

Method

1. Use the 12 scallop shells for the cooking and serving dishes. Mix the scallops with the sherry, and then place one scallop in each shell. Set aside.

2. Soak the black beans covered in cold water for 15 minutes, then rinse, dry on paper towels, and mince. Combine the beans, garlic, soy sauce, salt, pepper, sugar, oil and cornflour. Distribute some of this mixture equally over each of the scallops, and trickle the sesame oil over each.

3. Bring a few inches of water to a vigorous boil in a steamer. Place the scallops on a steamer rack, cover tightly, and steam for 5 minutes. Remove, sprinkle with spring onions, and garnish with one coriander leaf and a hot chilli diamond before serving.

SQUID
(Arrow, Asian, Californian, Mitre, Southern Calamary, Northern Calamary)

The squid has 10 tentacles encircling a parrot-like beak and a delicate quill-backbone. Squid has become a popular seafood, mainly as 'calamari', the widely available rings, normally sold deep-fried.

Availability: Sold whole, in rings, or tube-form. Also available prepared in breadcrumbs ready for cooking. Fresh, frozen or chilled.

Storage: Clean before storing, and refrigerate wrapped in GLAD Wrap or airtight GLAD Snap Lock Bags. Will keep up to 3 days in refrigerator and will store in freezer for up to 3 months.

Preparation: See preparation methods for squid on page 11.

Cooking: Cook whole or in rings. Most popular method is deep-fried. Coat in flour or batter, and fry in hot oil for 1–2 minutes. Serve with a dipping sauce.

Sautéed Calamari

(photographed page 83)

Ingredients
3 tablespoons olive oil
1 large onion (sliced)
2 teaspoons MasterFoods Freshly Crushed Garlic
1 tablespoon MasterFoods Sweet Basil Leaves
1 tablespoon MasterFoods Madras Mild Curry
salt and freshly ground MasterFoods Black Peppercorns
2 tablespoons honey
500g calamari rings
1 tablespoon MasterFoods Parsley Flakes

Method
1. Heat oil on barbecue plate, add onion and garlic, and sauté until tender.
2. Stir in basil, curry paste, salt, pepper and honey. Mix well.
3. Add the calamari rings, gently stir the calamari a few minutes (until cooked through). Stir in parsley.

Serves 4

Squid in Garlic Tomato Sauce

Ingredients
2 tablespoons olive oil
3 teaspoons MasterFoods Freshly Crushed Garlic
1 onion (chopped)
2 MasterFoods Bay Leaves
500g squid-hoods (cut into rings)
3 tomatoes (peeled and chopped)
1 tablespoon MasterFoods Tomato Paste
85mL dry white wine
85mL water

Method
1. Heat oil in frying pan, add garlic, onion and bay leaves, and cook, stirring (until onion is soft). Add squid, and cook, stirring, for about 3 minutes.
2. Stir-in tomatoes, tomato paste, wine and water. Bring to the boil. Cover and simmer gently for about 15 minutes (or until squid is tender).
3. Remove bay leaves before serving.

Serves 4

Squid with Celery, Carrot and Chinese Mushrooms

Ingredients
4 x dried Chinese mushrooms or shiitake
400g squid-mantles and tentacles (cleaned)
½ teaspoon salt
⅛ teaspoon MasterFoods Ground White Pepper
½ teaspoon sesame oil
½ teaspoon chilli oil
2 teaspoons cornflour
2 tablespoons corn oil
¼ teaspoon MasterFoods Freshly Chopped Ginger
3–4 stalks celery (sliced diagonally into 2.5cm pieces)
2 shallots (cut diagonally into 2cm pieces)
2 tablespoons dry sherry
125mL basic fish stock (page 39)
1 carrot (cut into thin decorative slices)
1 teaspoon cornflour mixed with 1 tablespoon cold water

Method
1. Soak the mushrooms in warm water for 30 minutes. Then drain, pressing out the excess water. Cut-off and discard the tough stems, and slice each cap into thirds. Set aside.
2. Cut the squid-mantles lengthwise along one side to open them. Score the inside surface diagonally with a sharp knife (about ¾ of the way through) at 50mm intervals.
3. Turn the squid a quarter-turn, and score again (to form a diagonal cross-hatch pattern). Then cut each mantle along the score-lines into 2cm strips. Trim and discard the two longest tentacles and keep the rest of the tentacles whole.
4. In a small bowl, mix the salt, pepper, sesame and chilli oils and cornflour, Add the squid, toss to coat well and set aside.
5. Heat a wok or 30cm skillet over high heat, add 1 tablespoon of the corn oil, add the squid, and stir-fry until just evenly opaque (about 30 seconds). Transfer squid to a plate and add the remaining oil to pan. When hot, add the ginger and stir-fry (until fragrant), then add the celery, shallots and mushrooms and stir-fry for 2 minutes.
6. Add the sherry, stock and carrots, cover, and cook for 1 minute more.
7. Stir the cornflour and add it, continuing to cook until the sauce boils and thickens slightly (about 30 seconds longer).
8. Transfer to a serving dish and serve immediately

Serves 4

Sautéed Calamari

Recommended Marinades

Oranges & Lemons Marinade
(Suitable for barbequed, grilled or baked fish)

Ingredients

2 tablespoons MasterFoods Soy sauce
2 tablespoons fresh orange juice
1 tablespoon olive oil
1 teaspoon lemon zest
1 tablespoon lemon juice
2 tablespoons MasterFoods Tomato Paste
1 teaspoon MasterFoods Freshly Crushed Garlic
½ teaspoon MasterFoods Basil Leaves
½ teaspoon MasterFoods Ground Oregano Leaves

Method

1. Combine all ingredients in a shallow dish. Stir well to combine.
2. Place fish in dish and allow to marinate in refrigerator for a minimum of one hour.
3. When cooking, baste fish frequently with marinade.

Makes about 125mL

Chilli Lime Marinade
(Suitable for Orange Roughy, Snapper or Tuna)

Ingredients

2 fresh jalapeno chillies (seeded and stemmed)
2 teaspoons MasterFoods Crushed Garlic
125mL balsamic vinegar
4 tablespoons freshly squeezed lime juice
2 tablespoons light olive oil
¼ teaspoon Masterfoods Ground Cumin seeds
½ teaspoon MasterFoods Soy Sauce
¼ teaspoon MasterFoods Freshly Ground Black Pepper
¼ teaspoon honey

Method

1. Place all ingredients in a blender or food processor and blend to a purée.
2. Place fish in a shallow dish, pour the purée over the fish and allow to marinate for at least an hour, in the refrigerator.
3. When cooking, baste fish frequently with the marinade.

Makes about 125mL

Garlic & Yogurt Marinade
(Suitable for grilled or barbecued fish steaks)

Ingredients

250g plain yogurt
125mL olive oil
2 tablespoons fresh lemon juice
2 teaspoons MasterFoods Freshly Crushed Garlic
2 teaspoons MasterFoods Parsley Flakes
½ teaspoon MasterFoods Basil Leaves
½ teaspoon MasterFoods Tarragon Leaves

Method

1. Place all ingredients in a blender or food processor and blend to a purée.
2. Place fish in a shallow dish, pour the purée over the fish and allow to marinate for at least an hour, in the refrigerator.
3. When cooking, brush fish frequently with the marinade

Makes about 190mL

Ginger-It-Up Marinade

Ingredients

1 teaspoon MasterFoods Freshly Minced Ginger
2 tablespoons MasterFoods Soy Sauce
65mL freshly squeezed lemon juice
1 tablespoon MasterFoods Dijon Mustard
1 tablespoon honey

Method

1. Combine all ingredients in a shallow dish. Stir well to combine. (It may be easier to blend if the honey is warmed slightly.)
2. Place fish in a shallow dish, pour the purée over the fish and allow to marinate for at least an hour, in the refrigerator.
3. When cooking, baste fish frequently with marinade.

Makes about 125mL

Court Bouillon
(For poaching fish)

Ingredients

1.25 litres water
1 large carrot (diced)
1 medium onion (diced)
1 stick celery (diced)
1 MasterFoods Bay Leaf
½ teaspoon MasterFoods Basil Leaves
½ teaspoon MasterFoods Tarragon Leaves
½ teaspoon MasterFoods Peppercorns
½ teaspoon MasterFoods Parsley Flakes
4 tablespoons freshly squeezed lemon juice
½ teaspoon salt

Method

1. Place all ingredients in a non-aluminium pan. Bring to simmer and brew for about 10 minutes, uncovered. Allow to cool.
2. Strain, and use as required. Freeze excess in refrigerator.

Makes about 1 litre

Honey Marinade
(Suitable for barbecued or grilled fillets)

Ingredients

3 tablespoons honey
1 tablespoon lemon zest
1 teaspoon MasterFoods Teriyaki Sauce
1 teaspoon MasterFoods Chilli Powder
1 teaspoons MasterFoods Freshly Minced Ginger
1 tablespoon freshly squeezed orange juice
3 shallots (finely chopped)
MasterFoods Freshly Ground Black Pepper to taste

Method

1. Place all ingredients in a non-aluminium pan, and heat gently until honey has melted through.
2. Place fish in a shallow dish, pour the purée over the fish and allow to marinate for at least an hour, in the refrigerator.
3. Place fish on griller or lightly oiled barbecue-plate. Cook on medium heat whilst basting fish frequently with marinade. (Fish will be cooked in about 3 minute each side.)

Makes about 125mL

Your recipes may require certain characteristics in the seafood you buy; for example, a firm texture, high oiliness or a low price. If the species recommended in the recipe is unavailable, you may use these tables to find an alternative species.

Species	Where Caught/Harvested							When Caught/Harvested												Wild/Farmed		Habitat			Flavour			Oiliness			Moisture			Texture			Shape (fillet)		
	NSW	Qld	Vic	WA	Tas	SA	NT	January	February	March	April	May	June	July	August	September	October	November	December	Wild	Farmed	Saltwater	Estuarine	Freshwater	Mild	Medium	Strong	Low	Medium	High	Dry	Medium	Moist	Soft	Medium	Firm	Thick	Medium	Thin
Atlantic Salmon					●			●	●	●	●			●	●	●	●	●	●		●	●		●	●	●				●			●		●		●		
Barramundi		●		●		●	●	●	●	●	●	●	●	●	●	●	●	●	●	●	●	●	●		●			◐	●	◐			●		●	●	●		
Blue Eye	●		●		●	●		●	●	▲	▲	▲	▲	▲	▲	▲	▲	▲		●		●			●				◐	◐			●				●	●	
Blue Grenadier	●		●		●	●		▲	▲	▲	▲	▲	●	●	●	●	▲	▲	▲	■		●			●			◐	◐			●	◐	◐					●	
Bream	●	●	●	●		●		●	●	●	●	●	●	●	●	●	●	●	●	●		●	●		●			◐	◐			●	◐	◐					●
Coral Trout		●		●			●	▲	▲	▲	●	●	●	●	●	●	●	●	▲	●		●			●			◐	◐			●				●	●		
Dory	●		●					▲	▲	▲	▲	▲	●	●	▲	▲	▲	●		●		●			●			◐	◐			●	●						●
Eel	●	●	●		●			●	▲	▲	▲	▲	▲	▲	▲	▲	▲	●		●	▲		●	●	●				●		●				●			◐	◐
Emperor		●		●			●	●	▲	▲	▲	▲	▲	▲	▲	▲	▲	▲	●	●		●			●				●				●			●	●		
Flathead	●	●	●	●	●	●	●	●	●	●	●	●	▲	▲	▲	▲	■	●	●	●						●		●					●	●	●	●		●	
Flounder	●	●	●	●		●		●	●	▲	▲	▲	▲	▲	▲	▲	▲	●		●		●	●			●		●				●				●			●
Freshwater Finfish	●		●			●		●	●	●	●	●	●	●	●	●	●	●	●	●	▲			●	●	●	●	◐	◐		●	●	●	●	●		●	●	●
Garfish	●	●	●	●	●	●		●	●	▲	▲	▲	▲	▲	▲	▲	▲	●		●		●	●	●		●		◐	◐			●		●	◐	◐			●
Kingfish	●			●				●	●	●	●	●	●	●	●	●	●	●		●			●			●		◐	●	◐	◐	◐			◐	◐	●		
Leatherjacket					●			●	●	▲	▲	▲	▲	▲	▲	▲	▲	●		●			●		●							●				●		◐	◐
Ling	●		●		●	●		▲	▲	▲	▲	▲	●	●	●	▲	▲	▲		●			●			●		◐	◐				●			●			
Mackerel	●	●		●			●	●	●	●	●	●	●	●	●	●	●	●	●	●			●				●	◐	◐	◐	◐				◐	◐	●		
Morwong	●		●	●	●	●		●	●	●	●	●	▲	▲	▲	▲	▲	●		●			●				●	◐	◐			●			◐	◐		●	
Mullet	●	●	●	●		●		▲	●	●	●	●	●	●	●	●	▲	▲	▲	●		▲	●				●	◐	◐			●		●	◐	◐			●
Mulloway	●	●	●		●			●	●	▲	▲	▲	▲	▲	▲	■	■	●		●			●			●			●				●		●	●			
Orange Roughy		●	●	●									●	●	●					●			●			●		◐	◐			●			◐	◐		◐	
Oreo					●			●	●	●	●	●	●	●	●	●	●	●	●	●			●			●			●			●			●				●
Rainbow Trout	●		●	●	●	●		●	●	●	●	●	●	●	●	●	●	●	●		●			●	◐	◐				●		●	●				◐	◐	
Red Emperor		●		●			●	●	●	●	●	●	●	●	●	●	●	●	●	●			●		●			●				●				●	●		
Redfish	●					●		▲	▲	▲	▲	▲	▲	▲	●	●	●	▲		●		●				●		◐	◐			●		◐	◐				
Rock Cod		●		●		●		●	●	●	●	●	●	●	●	●	●	●	●	●		●	●		●			●				●				●	●		
Shark	●	●	●	●	●	●	●	●	●	●	●	●	●	●	●	●	●	●	●	●						●		●				●			◐	◐	●		
Snapper	●	●	●	●		●		▲	▲	▲	▲	▲	●	●	●	▲	▲	▲	●	●	●	●	●		●			◐	◐			●			●		◐	◐	
Tailor	●	●	●	●									●	●	●					●			●				●		●				●		●	◐	◐		◐
Threadfin		●		●			●	▲	▲	▲	▲	●	●	●	●	▲	▲	▲		●		●	●			●		●				●				●	●		
Trevally	●	●		●				●	●	▲	▲	▲	▲	▲	▲	▲	●	●		●			●				●	◐	◐	●				◐	◐	●			
Tropical Snapper					●	●	●	●	●	●	●	●	●	●	●	●	●	●	●	●		●			◐	◐				●			●			●	●		
Tuna	●	●	●			●		●	●	●	●	●	●	●	●	●	●	●	●	●	●				●	●		◐	◐	◐	◐			◐	●	◐	◐		
Warehou	●		●		●	●		●	●				●	●				●		●			●			●		◐	◐	◐	◐				●		●		
Westralian Jewfish and Pearl Perch	●	●		●				●	●	●	●	●	●	●	●	▲	▲	▲	●	●			●		●			◐	◐			●	●		●		●		
Whiting	●		●	●		●		●	●	●	●	●	●	●	●	●	●	●	●	●			●	●	●			●				●		●	●	●		●	

Triangles indicate that only some of the species fulfil this characteristic.
Squares indicate that most of the species fulfil this characteristic.
Half-circles indicate a mid-range of the characteristic; for example, King Prawn's (top right, below) texture is Medium to Firm.

Species	Where Caught/Harvested							When Caught/Harvested												Wild/Farmed		Habitat			Flavour			Oiliness			Moisture			Texture		
	NSW	Qld	Vic	WA	Tas	SA	NT	January	February	March	April	May	June	July	August	September	October	November	December	Wild	Farmed	Saltwater	Estuarine	Freshwater	Mild	Medium	Strong	Low	Medium	High	Dry	Medium	Moist	Soft	Medium	Firm
King Prawn	●	●	●	●		●	●	●	●	●	●	●	●	●	●	●	●	●	●	●	▲	●	●			●		●					●		◗	◖
Banana Prawn		●		●			●			●	●	●								●		●			●			●					●		●	
Tiger Prawn	●	●		●		●	●	●	●	●	●	●	●	●	●	●	●	●	●	●	●	●				●		●					●		◗	◖
Endeavour Prawn		●		●		●	●	●	●	●	▲	▲	▲	▲	▲	▲	▲	▲	●	●		●			◗	◖		●					●			●
School Prawn	●	●	●	●				●	▲	▲	▲	▲	▲	●	●	●	●	●	●	●		●	●		●			●					●		●	
Bay Prawn	●	●						●	▲	▲	▲	▲	▲	●	●	●	●	●	●	●		●	●		●			●					●			●
Mud Crab	●	●		●		●	●	●	●	●	●	●	●	●	●	●	●	●	●	●		●			◗	◖		●					●		●	●
Spanner Crab	●	●							▲	▲	▲	▲	▲	▲	▲	●	●	▲	▲	●		●				●		●					●	●	●	
Blue Swimmer Crab		●		●		●		▲	●	●	●	●	▲	▲	▲	▲	▲			●		●	●		●			●					●			●
Bug	●	●		●		●	●	●	●	●	●	●	●	●	●	●	●	●	●	●		●			◗	◖		●					●			●
Rock Lobster	●	●	●	●	●	●	●	●	●	●	●	●	●	●	●	●	●	●	●	●		●				●		●					●		◗	◖
Freshwater Crayfish																					●			●	●			●					●			●
Yabby	●		●	●		●		●	●	●	●					●	●	●	●	▲	●															
Red Claw		●							●	●	●	●	●	●	●	●	●	●			●															
Marron				●		●		●	●	●	●	●	●	▲	▲	▲	▲	▲	●		●															
Abalone								●	●	●	●	●	●	●	●	●	●	●	●	●	●	▲				●		●				●				●
Blacklip abalone (flesh only)	●		●	●	●	●																														
Greenlip abalone (flesh only)			●	●	●	●																														
Scallop																						●						●	●			●				
Southern Scallop	●		●	●				●	●	●	●	●	●	●	●	●	●	●	●	●	▲														●	
Saucer Scallop		●		●				●	●	●	●	●	●	●	▲	▲	▲	●	●	●																●
Oyster								●	●	●	●	●	●	●	●	●	●	●	●		●		●			●	●					●	●			
Sydney Rock Oyster	●	●	●																																	
Pacific Oyster	●				●	●																														
Mussel								●	●	●	●	●	●	●	▲	▲	▲	●	●	▲	●	●						●	●				●	●		
Blue Mussel	●		●	●	●																															
Green Mussel																																				
Squid	●	●	●	●	●	●	●	●	●	●	●	●	●	●	●	●	●	●	●	●		●			●			●			●					●
Southern Calamary																																				
Arrow Squid																																				
Octopus	●		●	●	●	●		●	●	●	●	●	●	●	●	●	●	●	●	●		●			●			●			●					●

Weights & Measures

Cooking is not an exact science: one does not require finely calibrated scales, pipettes and scientific equipment to cook, but the conversion to metric measures in some countries, and its interpretation, must have intimidated many a good cook.

Weights are given in the recipes only for ingredients such as meats, fish, poultry and some vegetables. However, a few grams or ounces one way or another will not affect the success of your dish.

Although recipes have been tested using the Australian Standard 250mL cup, 20mL tablespoon and 5mL teaspoon, they will work just as well with the US and Canadian 8 fluid ounce cup, or the UK 300mL cup. We have used graduated cup measures (in preference to tablespoon measures) so that proportions are always the same. Where tablespoon measures have been given, these are not crucial measures, so using the smaller tablespoon of the US or UK will not affect the success of the recipe. At least we all agree on the teaspoon size.

For breads, cakes, pastries, etc., the only area which might cause concern is where eggs are used, as proportions will then vary. If working with a 250mL or 300mL cup, use large eggs (60g or 2 oz), adding a little more liquid to the recipe for 300mL cup measures if it seems necessary. Use the medium-sized eggs (55g or 1¼oz) with a 8 fl oz cup measure. A graduated set of measuring cups and spoons is recommended, the cups, in particular, being recommended for measuring dry ingredients. Remember to level such ingredients.

ENGLISH AND AMERICAN MEASURES

ENGLISH
All measurements are similar to Australian with two exceptions: (i) the English cup measures 10 fluid ounces (300mL), whereas the Australian cup measures 8 fluid ounces (250mL); and (ii) the English tablespoon (the Australian dessertspoon) measures 14.8mL against the Australian tablespoon of 20mL.

AMERICAN
The American reputed pint is 16 fluid ounces, a quart is equal to 32 fluid ounces, and the American gallon is 128 fluid ounces. The Imperial measurement is 20 fluid ounces to the pint, 40 fluid ounces to the quart, and 160 fluid ounces to one gallon. The American tablespoon is equal to 14.8mL, and the teaspoon is 5mL. The cup measure is 8 fluid ounces (250mL), the same as Australia.

DRY MEASURES

All the measures are level, so when you have filled a cup or spoon, level it off with the edge of a knife.

The scale below is the 'cook's equivalent', *and is not an exact conversion of metric to imperial measurement.*

The exact metric equivalent is 2.2046 lb = 1kg
or 1 lb = 0.45359kg

METRIC		IMPERIAL	
g = grams		oz = ounces	
kg = kilograms		lb = pound	
15g		½ oz	
20g		⅔ oz	
30g		1 oz	
60g		2 oz	
90g		3 oz	
125g		4 oz	¼ lb
155g		5 oz	
185g		6 oz	
220g		7 oz	
250g		8 oz	½ lb
280g		9 oz	
315g		10 oz	
345g		11 oz	
375g		12 oz	¾ lb
410g		13 oz	
440g		14 oz	
470g		15 oz	
1000g	1kg	35.2 oz	2.2 lb
	1.5kg		3.3 lb

OVEN TEMPERATURES

The Celsius temperatures given here are not exact; they have been rounded off and are given as a guide only. Follow the manufacturer's temperature guide, relating it to oven description given in the recipe. Remember gas ovens are hottest at the top, electric ovens at the bottom and convection fan-forced ovens are usually even throughout. We include Regulo numbers for gas cookers which may assist. To convert °C to °F multiply °C by 9 and divide by 5, then add 32.

	°C	°F	REGULO
Very slow	120	250	1
Slow	150	300	2
Moderately slow	150	325	3
Moderate	180	350	4
Moderately hot	190–200	370–400	5–6
Hot	210–220	410–440	6–7
Very hot	230	450	8
Super hot	250–290	475–500	9–10

CAKE DISH SIZES

METRIC	IMPERIAL
15cm	6"
18cm	7"
20cm	8"
23cm	9"

LOAF DISH SIZES

METRIC	IMPERIAL
23cm x 12cm	9" x 5"
25cm x 8cm	10" x 3"
28cm x 18cm	11" x 7"

LIQUID MEASURES

METRIC mL millilitres	IMPERIAL fl oz fluid ounce	CUP & SPOON
5mL	⅙ fl oz	1 teaspoon
20mL	⅔ fl oz	1 tablespoon
30mL	1 fl oz	1 tablespoon plus 2 teaspoons
60mL	2 fl oz	¼ cup
85mL	2½ fl oz	⅓ cup
100mL	3 fl oz	⅜ cup
125mL	4 fl oz	½ cup
150mL	5 fl oz	¼ pint, 1 gill
250mL	8 fl oz	1 cup
300mL	10 fl oz	½ pint
360mL	12 fl oz	1½ cups
420mL	14 fl oz	1¾ cups
500mL	16 fl oz	2 cups
600mL	20 fl oz	1 pint, 2½ cups
1 litre	35 fl oz	1¾ pints, 4 cups

CUP MEASUREMENTS

One cup is equal to the following weights.

	METRIC	IMPERIAL
Almonds, flaked	90g	3 oz
Almonds, slivered, ground	125g	4 oz
Almonds, kernels	155g	5 oz
Apples, dried, chopped	125g	4 oz
Apricots, dried, chopped	190g	6 oz
Breadcrumbs, packet	125g	4 oz
Breadcumbs, soft	60g	2 oz
Cheese, grated	125g	4 oz
Choc Bits	155g	5 oz
Coconut, desiccated	90g	3 oz
Cornflakes	30g	1 oz
Currants	155g	5 oz
Flour	125g	4 oz
Fruit, dried (mixed, sultanas etc.)	185g	6 oz
Ginger, crystallised, glacé	250g	8 oz
Honey, treacle, golden syrup	315g	10 oz
Mixed Peel	220g	7 oz
Nuts, chopped	125g	4 oz
Prunes, chopped	220g	7 oz
Rice, cooked	155g	5 oz
Rice, uncooked	185g	6 oz
Rolled Oats	90g	3 oz
Sesame Seeds	125g	4 oz
Shortening (butter, margarine)	250g	8 oz
Sugar, brown	155g	5 oz
Sugar, granulated or caster	250g	8 oz
Sugar, sifted icing	155g	5 oz
Wheat germ	60g	2 oz

LENGTH

Some of us are still having trouble converting imperial to metric. In this scale measures have been rounded off to the easiest-to-use and most acceptable figures.

To obtain the exact metric equivalent to convert inches to centimetres, multiply inches by 2.54

Therefore 1 inch equals 25.4 millimetres and 1 millimetre equals 0.03937 inches

METRIC mm = millimetres cm = centimetres	IMPERIAL in = inches ft = feet
5mm (0.5cm)	¼ in
10mm (1.0cm)	½ in
20mm (2.0cm)	¾ in
25mm (2.5cm)	1 in
50mm (5cm)	2 in
80mm (8cm)	3 in
100mm (10cm)	4 in
120mm (12cm)	5 in
150mm (15cm)	6 in
180mm (18cm)	7 in
200mm (20cm)	8 in
230mm (23cm)	9 in
250mm (25cm)	10 in
280mm (28cm)	11 in
300mm (30cm)	1 ft (12 in)

Glossary

acidulated water: water with added acid, such as lemon juice or vinegar, which prevents discolouration of ingredients, particularly fruit or vegetables; the proportion of acid to water is 1 teaspoon per 300mL

al dente: Italian cooking term for ingredients that are cooked until tender but still firm to the bite; usually applied to pasta

americaine: method of serving seafood—usually lobster and monkfish—in a sauce flavoured with olive oil, aromatic herbs, tomatoes, white wine, fish stock, brandy and tarragon

an glaise: cooking style for simple cooked dishes such as boiled vegetables; assiette an glaise is a plate of cold cooked meats

antipasto: Italian for 'before the meal'; it denotes an assortment of cold meats, vegetables and cheeses, often marinated, served as an hors d'œuvre; a typical antipasto might include salami, prosciutto, marinated artichoke hearts, anchovy fillets, olives, tuna fish and Provolone cheese

au gratin: food sprinkled with breadcrumbs, often covered with cheese sauce and browned until a crisp coating forms

balsamic vinegar: a mild, extremely fragrant wine-based vinegar made in northern Italy; traditionally, the vinegar is aged for at least seven years in a series of casks made of various woods

baste: to moisten food while it is cooking by spooning or brushing on liquid or fat

baine marie: a saucepan standing in a large pan which is filled with boiling water to keep liquids at simmering point; a double boiler will do the same job

beat: to stir thoroughly and vigourously

beurre manie: equal quantities of butter and flour kneaded together and added a little at a time to thicken a stew or casserole

bird: *see* **paupiette**

blanc: a cooking liquid made by adding flour and lemon juice to water in order to keep certain vegetables from discolouring as they cook

blanch: to plunge into boiling water and then (in some cases) into cold water; fruits and nuts are blanched to remove skin easily

blanquette: a white stew of lamb, veal or chicken, bound with egg yolks and cream, and accompanied by onion and mushrooms

blend: to mix thoroughly

bonne femme: dishes cooked in the traditional French 'housewife' style; chicken and pork *bonne femme* are garnished with bacon, potatoes and baby onion; fish *bonne femme* with mushrooms in a white wine sauce

bou guet garni: a bunch of herbs, usually consisting of sprigs of parsley, thyme, marjoram, rosemary, a bayleaf, peppercorns and cloves, tied in muslin and used to flavour stews and casseroles

braise: to cook whole or large pieces of poultry, game, fish, meat or vegetables in a small amount of wine, stock or other liquid in a closed pot; often the main ingredient is first browned in fat and then cooked in a low oven or very slowly on top of the stove; braising suits tough meats and older birds, and produces a mellow, rich sauce

broil: the American term for grilling food

brown: to cook in a small amount of fat until brown

bulgur: a type of cracked wheat in which the kernels are steamed and dried before being cracked

buttered: to spread with softened or melted butter

butterfly: to slit a piece of food in half horizontally, cutting it almost through so that when opened it resembles butterfly wings; chops, large prawns and thick fish fillets are often butterflied so that they cook more quickly

buttermilk: a tangy, low-fat cultured milk product the slight acidity of which makes it an ideal marinade base for poultry

calzone: a semicircular pocket of pizza dough, stuffed with meat or vegetables, sealed and baked

caramelise: to melt sugar until it is a golden brown syrup

champignons: small mushrooms, usually canned

chasseur: (hunter) a French cooking style in which meat and chicken dishes are cooked with mushrooms, shallots, white wine, and often tomato

clarify: to melt butter and drain the oil off the sediment

coat: to cover with a thin layer of flour, sugar, nuts, crumbs, poppy or sesame seeds, cinnamon sugar or a few of the ground spices

concasser: to chop coarsely, usually tomatoes

confit: from the French verb *confire*, meaning to preserve; refers to food that is made into a preserve by cooking very slowly and thoroughly until tender; in the case of meat (such as duck or goose) it is cooked in its own fat, and covered with it, so that it does not come into contact with the air; vegetables such as onions are good in *confit*

consommé: a clear soup usually made from beef

coulis: a thin purée, usually of fresh or cooked fruit or vegetables, which is soft enough to pour (*couler* means to run); a coulis may be rough-textured or very smooth

court bouillon: the liquid in which fish, poultry or meat is cooked; it usually consists of water with bayleaf, onion, carrots and salt (and freshly ground black pepper to taste); other additives can include wine, vinegar, stock, garlic or spring onions (scallions)

couscous: cereal processed from semolina into pellets, traditionally steamed and served with meat and vegetables in the classic North African stew of the same name

cruciferous vegetables: certain members of the mustard, cabbage and turnip families with cross-shaped flowers and strong aromas and flavours

cream: to make soft, smooth and creamy by rubbing with back of spoon or by beating with mixer; usually applied to fat and sugar

croûtons: small toasted or fried cubes of bread

crudites: raw vegetables, whether cut in slices or sticks, to nibble plain or with a dipping sauce, or shredded and tossed as salad with a simple dressing

cube: to cut into small pieces with 6 equal sides

curdle: to cause milk or sauce to separate into solid and liquid (for example, overcooked egg mixtures)

daikon radish: (also called mooli): a long white Japanese radish

dark sesame oil: (also called Oriental sesame oil): dark polyunsaturated oil with a low burning point, used for seasoning; (do not replace with lighter sesame oil)

deglaze: to dissolve congealed cooking juices or glaze on the bottom of a pan by adding a liquid, then scraping and stirring vigourously whilst bringing the liquid to the boil; juices may be used to make gravy or to add to sauce

degrease: to skim grease from the surface of liquid; if possible the liquid should be chilled so the fat solidifies; if not, skim off most of the fat with a large metal spoon, then trail strips of paper towel on the surface of the liquid to remove any remaining globules

devilled: a dish or sauce that is highly seasoned with a hot ingredient such as mustard, Worcestershire sauce or cayenne pepper

dice: to cut into small cubes

dietary-fibre: a plant-cell material that is undigested or only partially digested in the human body, but which promotes healthy digestion of other food matter

dissolve: mix a dry ingredient with liquid until absorbed

dredge: to coat with a dry ingredient, such as flour or sugar

drizzle: to pour in a fine thread-like stream over a surface

dust: to sprinkle or coat lightly with flour or icing sugar

Dutch oven: a heavy casserole with a lid, usually made from cast iron or pottery

emulsion: a mixture of two liquids that are not mutually soluble—for example, oil and water

entrée: in Europe, the 'entry' or hors d'œuvre; in North America entrée means the main course

fillet: special cut of beef, lamb, pork or veal; breast of poultry and game; fish cut off the bone lengthways

flake: to break into small pieces with a fork

flame: to ignite warmed alcohol over food

fold-in: a gentle, careful combining of a light or delicate mixture with a heavier mixture using a metal spoon

fricassee: a dish in which poultry, fish or vegetables are bound together with a white or veloute sauce; in Britain and the United States, the name applies to an old-fashioned dish of chicken in a creamy sauce

galette: sweet or savoury mixture shaped as a flat round

garnish: to decorate food, usually with something edible

gastrique: caramelised sugar deglazed with vinegar and used in fruit-flavoured savoury sauces, in such dishes as duck with orange

glaze: a thin coating of beaten egg, syrup or aspic which is brushed over pastry, fruits or cooked meats

gluten: a protein in flour that is developed when dough is kneaded, making it elastic

gratin: a dish cooked in the oven or under the grill so that it develops a brown crust; bread crumbs or cheese may be sprinkled on top first; shallow gratin dishes ensure a maximum area of crust

grease: to rub or brush lightly with oil or fat

joint: to cut poultry, game or small animals into serving pieces by dividing at the joint

julienne: to cut food into match-like strips

knead: to work dough using the heel of the hand with a pressing motion, while stretching and folding the dough

line: to cover the inside of a container with paper, to protect or aid in removing mixture

infuse: to immerse herbs, spices or other flavourings in hot liquid to flavour it; infusion takes 2–5 minutes depending on the flavouring; the liquid should be very hot but not boiling

jardiniere: a garnish of garden vegetables, typically carrots, pickling onions, French beans and turnips

lights: lungs of an animal, used in various meat preparations such as pâtès and faggots

macerate: to soak food in liquid to soften

marinade: a seasoned liquid, usually an oil and acid mixture, in which meats or other foods are soaked to soften and give more flavour

marinara: Italian 'sailor's style' cooking that does not apply to any particular combination of ingredients; marinara tomato sauce for pasta is most familiar

marinate: to let food stand in a marinade to season and tenderise

mask: to cover cooked food with sauce

melt: to heat until liquified

mince: to grind into very small pieces

mix: to combine ingredients by stirring

monounsaturated fats: one of three types of fats found in foods; are believed not to raise the level of cholesterol in the blood

niçoise: a garnish of tomatoes, garlic and black olives; a salad with anchovy, tuna and French beans is typical

non-reactive pan: a cooking pan the surface of which does not chemically react with food; materials used include stainless steel, enamel, glass and some alloys

noisette: small 'nut' of lamb cut from boned loin or rack that is rolled, tied and cut in neat slices; noisette also means flavoured with hazel nuts, or butter cooked to a nut brown colour

normande: a cooking style for fish, with a garnish of shrimp, mussels and mushrooms in a white wine cream sauce; for poultry and meat, a sauce with cream, Calvados and apple

olive oil: various grades of oil extract from olives; extra virgin olive oil has a full, fruity flavour and the lowest acidity; virgin olive oil is slightly higher in acidity and lighter in flavour; pure olive oil is a processed blend of olive oils and has the highest acidity and lightest taste

panade: a mixture for binding stuffings and dumplings, notably *quenelles*, often of choux pastry or simply bread crumbs; a *panade* may also be made of *fran gipane*, puréed potatoes or rice

papillote: to cook food in oiled or buttered greasepoof paper or aluminium foil; also a decorative frill to cover bone ends of chops and poultry drumsticks

parboil: to boil or simmer until part-cooked (that is, cooked further than when blanching)

pare: to cut away outside covering

pâtè: a paste of meat or seafood used as a spread for toast or crackers

paupiette: a thin slice of meat, poultry or fish spread with a savoury stuffing and rolled; in the United States this is also called 'bird' and in Britain an 'olive'

peel: to strip away outside covering

plump: to soak in liquid or moisten thoroughly until full and round

poach: to simmer gently in enough hot liquid to cover, using care to retain shape of food

polyunsaturated fats: one of the three types of fats found in food; these exist in large quantities in such vegetable oils as safflower, sunflower, corn and soyabean; these fats lower the level of cholesterol in the blood

purée: a smooth paste, usually of vegetables or fruits, made by putting foods through a sieve, food mill or liquefying in a blender or food processor

ragout: traditionally a well-seasoned, rich stew containing meat, vegetables and wine; nowadays, a term applied to any stewed mixture

ramekins: small oval or round individual baking dishes

reconstitute: to put moisture back into dehydrated foods by soaking in liquid

reduce: to cook over a very high heat, uncovered, until the liquid is reduced by evaporation

refresh: to cool hot food quickly, either under running water or by plunging it into iced water, to stop it cooking; particularly for vegetables and occasionally for shellfish

rice vinegar: mild, fragrant vinegar that is less sweet than cider vinegar and not as harsh as distilled malt vinegar; Japanese rice vinegar is milder than the Chinese variety

roulade: a piece of meat, usually pork or veal, that is spread with stuffing, rolled and often braised or poached; a roulade may also be a sweet or savoury mixture that is baked in a Swiss roll tin or paper case, filled with a contrasting filling, and rolled

rubbing-in: a method of incorporating fat into flour, by use of fingertips only; also incorporates air into mixture

safflower oil: the vegetable oil that contains the highest proportion of polyunsaturated fats

salsa: a juice derived from the main ingredient being cooked or a sauce added to a dish to enhance its flavour; in Italy the term is often used for pasta sauces; in Mexico the name usually applies to uncooked sauces served as an accompaniment, especially to corn chips

saturated fats: one of the three types of fats found in foods; these exist in large quantities in animal products, coconut and palm oils; they raise the level of cholesterol in the blood; as high cholesterol levels may cause heart disease, saturated fat consumption is recommended to be less than 15 per cent of kilojoules provided by the daily diet

sauté: to cook or brown in small amount of hot fat

score: to mark food with cuts, notches of lines to prevent curling or to make food more attractive

scald: to bring just to boiling point, usually for milk; also to rinse with boiling water

sear: to brown surface quickly over high heat in hot dish

seasoned flour: flour with salt and pepper added

sift: to shake a dry, powdered substance through a sieve or sifter to remove any lumps and give lightness

simmer: to cook food gently in liquid that bubbles steadily just below boiling point so that the food cooks in even heat without breaking up

singe: to quickly flame poultry to remove all traces of feathers after plucking

skim: to remove a surface layer (often of impurities and scum) from a liquid with a metal spoon or small ladle

slivered: sliced in long, thin pieces; usually refers to nuts, especially almonds

soften: re gelatine—sprinkle over cold water and allow to gel (soften) then dissolve and liquefy

souse: to cover food, particularly fish, in wine vinegar and spices and cook slowly; the food is cooled in the same liquid; sousing gives food a pickled flavour

steep: to soak in warm or cold liquid in order to soften food and draw out strong flavours or impurities

stir-fry: to cook thin slices of meat and vegetable over a high heat in a small amount of oil, stirring constantly to cook evenly in a short time; traditionally cooked in a wok, however a heavy-based frying pan may be used

stock: a liquid containing flavours, extracts and nutrients of bones, meat, fish or vegetables

stud: to adorn with; for example, baked ham studded with whole cloves

sugo: an Italian sauce made from the liquid or juice extracted from fruit or meat during cooking

sweat: to cook sliced or chopped food, usually vegetables, in a little fat and no liquid over very low heat; GLAD-Foil is pressed on top so that the food steams in its own juices, usually before being added to other dishes

timbale: a creamy mixture of vegetables or meat baked in a mould; French for 'kettle-drum'; also denotes a drum-shaped baking dish

thicken: to make a thin, smooth paste by mixing together arrowroot, cornflour or flour with an equal amount of cold water; stir into hot liquid, cook, stirring until thickened

toss: to gently mix ingredients with two forks or fork and spoon

total fat: the individual daily intake of all three fats previously described in this glossary; nutritionists recommend that fats provide no more than 35 per cent of the energy in the diet

vine leaves: tender, lightly flavoured leaves of the grapevine, used in ethnic cuisine as wrappers for savoury mixtures; as the leaves are usually packed in brine, they should be well rinsed before use

whip: to beat rapidly, incorporate air and produce expansion

zest: thin outer layer of citrus fruits containing the aromatic citrus oil; it is usually thinly pared with a vegetable peeler, or grated with a zester or grater to separate it from the bitter white pith underneath

Index

ACKNOWLEDGMENTS

The publishers wish to acknowledge and thank the following companies and individuals for the supply of products, recipes and props for photography in this book.

NationalPak Australia, for the supply of their marvellous range of GLAD products for use in our test kitchen and photographic studio. The publishers acknowledge that 'GLAD' is a registered trademark of NationalPak Australia Limited.

De Costi Seafoods, for the supply of their magnificent range of ocean-fresh fish and crustaceans, used in developing recipes, and for photography, in this book.

Jason Kent, Market Manager, MasterFoods of Australia for the supply of herbs and spices which were used in the preparation of food for photography and for use in the development of recipes and food testing in this book. The Publishers acknowledge the registered trademarks of Effem Foods Pty Ltd used in this book: MasterFoods; MasterFoods Cuisine Essentials.

Mr Doug Hamilton of McWilliams Wines for the supply of wines for recipe testing and photography and his advice and recommendation on type of wine to be consumed with specific seafood dishes. Robert Walters, for information supplied from his book; "R.I.Walters' Guide to Australian Wines".

Jan Wilson for assisting with the development of numerous tested recipes in this book. Di Kirby for providing a number of special recipes and for rewriting several.

Anthony Carroll and Kevin Kendall of The Fresh Ketch Restaurant, The Spit, Sydney, for providing the exceptionally tasty recipes on pages 14, 16 and 32 in this book.

Elizabeth Forest of Vancouver, Canada for her superb Bouillabaisse as shown on page 25 of this book.

Joanna Kane of Queensland Department of Primary Industries and the Fisheries Research and Development Corporation, for advice and assistance in the development of this book.

Nicola McConnell of the Sydney Fish Market for providing information, assistance and transparencies for this book.

For provision of props, china and glassware we thank the following: Villeroy and Boch, Brookvale, NSW and Waterford-Wedgewood, Castle Hill, NSW.

The recipes in this book have been compiled by the publisher, and supporting companies do not accept any responsibility for the contents of this book.

MAJOR CREDITS

Published by:
R&R Publishing Marketing Pty Ltd
ACN 083 612 579
PO Box 254 Carlton North Victoria 3054 Australia
Australia-wide Toll Free 1 800 063 296

© Richard Carroll
Publisher: Richard Carroll
Recipe Development: Ellen Argyriou, Jan Wilson, Di Kirby, Kevin Kendall
Computer Manager: Sean McNamara
Creative Director: Jon Terpstra
Photographer: Warren Webb
Stylist: Di Kirby
Assistants: Lyn Daines, Jenny Grainger and Sharyn Glover
Editor/Proof Reader: Rev. Dr Ross Gilham

The National Library of Australia
Cataloguing-in-Publication Data.
Fresh food cooking with seafood.
Includes index.
ISBN: 1 875655 61 1 (pbk)
ISBN: 1 875655 60 3 (case)
1. Cookery (Seafood). 2. (Series: Fresh food cooking).
641.692
First edition printed February 1998
This edition reprinted August 1998

Computer typeset in Bookman and Avant Garde by:
R&R Publishing Marketing Pty Ltd, Carlton North, Victoria, Australia
Film Scanning: PICA Overseas, Singapore
Printed in Singapore by: APP Printing, Singapore